AROUND THE WAY GIRL

AROUND THE WAY
GIRL

A Memoir

TARAJI P. HENSON
WITH DENENE MILLNER

37INK
—
ATRIA

New York   London   Toronto   Sydney   New Delhi

ATRIA BOOKS
An Imprint of Simon & Schuster, Inc.
1230 Avenue of the Americas
New York, NY 10020

First 37 Ink/Atria Books hardcover edition October 2016

37INK **/ ATRIA** BOOKS and colophon are trademarks of
Simon & Schuster, Inc.

For information about special discounts for bulk purchases,
please contact Simon & Schuster Special Sales at
1-866-506-1949 or business@simonandschuster.com.

The Simon & Schuster Speakers Bureau can bring authors to your live event. For
more information or to book an event, contact the Simon & Schuster Speakers
Bureau at 1-866-248-3049 or visit our website at www.simonspeakers.com.

Interior design by Dana Sloan

Manufactured in the United States of America

10 9 8 7 6 5 4 3 2 1

Library of Congress Cataloging-in-Publication Data has been applied for.

ISBN 978-1-5011-2599-7
ISBN 978-1-5011-2601-7 (ebook)

This book is dedicated to all of my angels watching over me.

R.I.P.
Boris Lawrence Henson
Madeline Henson
Russell Henson
Daniel Henson
George Henson
Gilbert Henson
Janie Sandle
Ricky Shields
Willie Ballard

Lineup

AROUND THE WAY GIRL

1

Fearless

Let my mother tell it, all that I am and all that I know is because of my daddy, a declaration that some might find shocking considering the list of negative attributes that floated like a dark cloud over my father's short, hard-lived life. During his fifty-eight years on this good, green earth, Boris Henson, born and reared in northeast DC, had been homeless and broke, an alcoholic and physically and mentally abusive to my mother during their five years together—plus prone to hot tempers and cool-off periods in the slammer. With that many strikes against his character, I can imagine that it's hard for some to see the good in who he was, much less how any comparison to him might be construed as a compliment. But Daddy wasn't average. Yes, there are plenty of fathers who, grappling with their demons, make the babies and leave the mamas and disappear like the wind, without a care in the world about the consequences. The scars run deep. That, however, is not my tale to tell. The truth is, no matter how loud the thunder created by his personal storms, my father always squared his shoulders, extended his arms, opened his heart, and did what was natural and right and beautiful—he loved me. My father's love was all at once regular and extraordinary, average and heroic. For starters, he was there. No matter his circumstances, no matter what kind of fresh hell he was dealing with or dishing out, he was there, even if he had to insist upon being a part of my life. One of my earliest memories of my dad is of him kidnapping me. It happened when I was about four years old, shortly after my father dragged my mother by her hair into his car while threatening to kill her. I'm told that the only thing that kept her from being dragged down the street with her body hanging out of his ride was my aunt's quick thinking: she pulled the keys out of the ignition before my father could speed away. He was angry because more than a week earlier, my mother, fearful that my father would follow through on a threat to kill her, packed up a few of our belongings in a brown paper bag and plotted a speedy getaway; she wanted to divorce him and bar him from seeing me until he got himself together and handled his bouts of addiction and anger. But my father wasn't having it. "Nothing and nobody was gonna keep me away from my baby girl," he used to tell me when he recounted the days when my mom and I disappeared. He said he even took to the top of buildings throughout our hardscrabble southeast DC neighborhood with binoculars to see if he could spot us. We were long gone, though, hiding out where he didn't think to look: back and forth between his parents' home in northeast DC and his sister's place in Nanjemoy, a small town in southern Maryland.

It took Dad more than a week to track us down at my aunt's

place, and when he finally made it over there, he waged war on her front door, banging and hollering like a madman, demanding to see me, his daughter.

"Let me see my baby!" he yelled. "Taraji! Come see your daddy!"

I was in the television room, which was in the back of the apartment, in a thin pair of pajamas, watching television and pulling a comb through my doll's hair when I heard my father screaming my name. That doll didn't have a chance; I left it, the comb, a brush, and a bowl of barrettes and baubles right there in the middle of the floor and started rooting around the recliner for my sneakers with the flowers on them when my mom, a naturally gorgeous cocoa beauty with a beautiful halo of hair, rushed into the room to check on me. "Come here," she said, scooping me up into her arms. She sat on the edge of the couch, rocking side to side; her palm, warm and slightly sweaty, pressed my head against her chest. The thud of her heartbeat tickled my ear.

. . .

I was much too young to understand the dynamics of my parents' relationship—that my mother was running for her life after he'd lost his temper one too many times and hit her. Nor did I understand that my father was violating my mother's wishes and scaring her half to death by dropping by unannounced and demanding time with me; all I knew was that my father was at the door and he wanted to play, that he would once again, as he always did, sprinkle magic on what would have been an average day. Try as she might and despite my aunt's pleas not to open the door, my mother couldn't ignore the scene Dad was making, the banging and screaming. He even left and came back with a police officer, someone my father, who was working as a cop at the time, knew on the force. To placate him and keep my aunt, I'm sure, from becoming the laughingstock of the neighborhood, my mother finally, slowly walked to the front door, with me in her arms. "Look," she said, seething, "you have got to stop it with all this noise. Please! You can see her for a few minutes, but then you have to go."

Dad, burly and strapping, standing at well over six feet tall, didn't give my mother a chance to put me in his arms; he snatched me and took off running into the winter chill, me dressed in nothing but those pajamas. Nothing could stop him—not my mother's screams, not the neighbors peering out their front doors and rushing down their driveways to get a glimpse of the Negro theater unfolding on the street, not threats from his fellow officer, who'd pointed his gun and considered shooting my father. Definitely not common sense. Where, after all, was he going to go? His home situation was sketchy, his money was funny, and really, the chance of him taking proper care of a four-year-old was slim to nil. Yet none of that mattered. He wanted to be with his daughter.

I thought we were about to go on one of the many fun and funny adventures we always embarked on together, whether that was going for a ride on his motorcycle or taking a walk in the park; never once did it cross my four-year-old mind that something was wrong—that we were like Bonnie and Clyde on the run. When Dad took off down the street, I wasn't scared; I was happy to be in his arms, so strong and thick and grand.

My father's getaway was short lived, though. "I'm going to

call the cops on your ass!" my mother yelled down the street after him as she and the police officer jumped in his cruiser. From the front seat of that cop car, my mother searched frantically for me and my father for hours, unaware that he'd stolen me away to a friend's house somewhere in the same neighborhood. It was my dad's friend who convinced him to let go of all that passion and make way for common sense: there was no way he'd be able to get away with stealing his daughter from his wife and he finally acknowledged that. Grudgingly, he brought me back to my pleading mother's waiting arms. "I'll come see you another time, baby girl," Dad said as my mother rushed away from him. "I love you. Daddy loves you. Don't you ever forget that."

What he did was wrong—I can see that now as an adult. Still I hold tight to my belief that at that time, my father was a good guy who simply wasn't very diplomatic about his wants and needs versus his rights, and a tad immature when it came to understanding how to get what he wanted from others. My mother was the one who would try to reason with him; she'd tell him time and again, "If you want full custody of your daughter, go to court and say, 'I'm her dad and I deserve rights, too.' But you don't come knock on the door and run off in the wind with our daughter, because that's not going to work. Get it together and we can talk."

. . .

As an adult, when I think of my parents' polar opposite personalities, I say to myself, *how in the hell did they ever meet?* She's quiet, thoughtful, methodical. He was loud and full of drama, quick to say and do the first thing to come to mind. He wasn't trying to hurt anybody; it's not as if he were robbing banks or knocking people upside the head and taking what was theirs. Quite the contrary: he was a Vietnam vet and an artist at heart, and when his finances were flush, he made good money as a metal fabricator, installing metal bars on the windows of houses throughout the metro DC area. But my father also was a victim of the lack of support provided for Vietnam vets who served their country, only to come home to a nation still reeling from political and racial turmoil, to say nothing of that shady Reaganomics math; the only thing that trickled down to him during the Reagan administration was a decrease in the lucrative contracts that sustained him financially. No one could afford window bars and fancy iron fences and front doors anymore, and when the middle class didn't have money, Dad didn't have money. Soon enough, the checks stopped coming and he couldn't pay the rent, at which point the entirety of his apartment was dumped out onto the street. Getting another job to keep a roof over his head was near impossible, as he had a record—a knot of misdemeanors he'd gotten for a couple of street fights made it difficult for him to secure a gig that would give him enough cash to live on. With no job, no money, and nowhere to go, he ended up living in the green van he was driving at the time.

Boris Henson was a lot of things, and he did a lot of things wrong, but he was a stand-up guy—a good guy who was dealing with the cards life dealt him, plenty of which would have ruined a lesser man. But what he chose to do with those hands is where the best life lessons for me lay. Rather than fold into a ball and disappear from my world, he turned all that ugly upside down and let me examine its underbelly. It was important to him that I see it all—the good and the tragic, the long, slow climb he made toward finding peace for himself—which he ultimately did when he got sober and found Jesus—and the pitfalls that threatened to swallow him whole along the way.

"Don't worry about that," he said of all the furniture and personal items he had to leave behind when he was evicted and living in his car. He cupped my face and looked me in my eyes. "That's material stuff I can get back. I'm alive. I'm free."

· · ·

I'm free. That's what mattered to him. And that's what mattered to me. There was so much emotional intelligence there, so many lessons for me to mine for my own life journey. Through example, he showed me that we're human—that nobody is perfect and there most certainly isn't a rulebook for living a perfect life. I was to train my eyes not on the misfortune, setbacks, or possibility of failure, but on living—really living—without fear. Time and again, my father would show me that no matter how often he fell from grace, he simply would not let the dread and anxiety of another failure shackle him. And how could he? He needed both of his hands free so that he could place them squarely on my back and push me forward past the fear.

The pushing started early, and my father showed no mercy, like the time he forced me to sink or swim, literally. His family, who generously arranged for me to attend all kinds of extracurricular activities my mother couldn't afford now that she was a single mom, paid for my swim lessons at an exclusive club in Capitol Hill, which might as well have been another world from the part of DC I called home. Every weekend, my mother would style my hair so pretty in little cornrows and dress me up in a cute bikini with an outfit and barrettes to match. Prancing, I'd kiss my mother good-bye, and while she walked over to the cordoned area behind the glass where the parents sat, I'd walk just as nice through the gym and out to the pool, as if I were eager to jump in the water. Then, as soon as I got to the pool, I'd take off running and screaming around the deck like somebody was trying to kill me. Terrified that I'd end up at the bottom of that sea of blue and chlorine, stuck like a brick to the pool floor, gasping and thrashing for air, I did not want to get in that water. Rather than toss myself into that liquid grave, I ran. Fast. So no one could catch me and force me into the pool. I was manipulative and slick— dramatic for no reason and drunk off the attention I got when I refused to listen to the swim teacher and instead employed my devil-may-care, run-like-the-white-girl-in-a-horror-movie antics. "Come on, sweetheart, just put your feet in the water," the instructor would insist every week as the rest of the class piled into the pool excitedly and I stood on the side, my arms folded, my brow furled, and my lip poked out. "You don't have to get all the way in just yet, but I want you to get used to the water. I won't let you go under, I promise. We'll take it slow." I'd take a step or two toward the pool, close enough for the teacher and her charges to *think* that maybe this week, I'd at least let the cool water hit my big toe. But I wasn't about to let that happen. Off I'd go, running. Dramatic, just like my father.

Every lesson, week in and week out, my mother would be completely embarrassed by my antics, and no amount of threatening or bribing could convince me to act any other way. Until, at her wits' end, my mother, unbeknownst to me, hipped my father to my game.

I'm at my next lesson, running and screaming around the pool, and who comes through the double glass pool doors but none other than Boris Lawrence Henson. I had just about finished my first lap around the perimeter of the pool when he walked in, practically in slow motion, looking like Shaft 2.0 in a leather trench coat and hat, fly as hell, mean mugging like he was about to get that work. He snatched me up by my arm, bent down, looked me dead in the eye, and let me have it. "You gonna sink or swim, do or die, but what you not gonna do is run around here acting crazy like somebody killing you." And then he did the unthinkable: he picked me up and tossed me into the water.

The water stopped splashing, every tongue fell silent, everybody froze in horror. This was not the place where you show up looking like a black superhero and then throw your daughter in the pool like "The Mack." But my father didn't give a damn. He zeroed right in on my drama. "Uh-huh, stay your ass in that water, too!" he yelled, jabbing his finger in my direction. "Your mother ain't driving you down here just for you to act like a little monkey!"

And when I hit that ice-cold water and it came splashing up all around my neck and eyes and nose and cornrows, what did Taraji Penda Henson learn to do that day?

Swim.

My dad saw all through my foolishness, latched on to my fear, and pulled it out of me. He was the muscle—the parent who, with one look, one curl of the lip, one phone call from my mother, could get me together and ensure I was on my best behavior and being brave. All my mother had to do was halfway say, "I'm going to call your father," and I'd see the light.

Thing is, my father never put his hands on me; he didn't have to. He simply knew how to bring out the best in me in a way that inspired me to expect the best out of myself. He managed this not so much by being strict but more so by trusting me, by encouraging me to trust myself. This was a recurring lesson that started as early as age seven, when my father started teaching me how to drive. I'd sit on his lap and steer his blue pickup truck through the back roads of Washington, DC, listening to the gravel grind and pop against the tires, giggling all the way. Sometimes, when it seemed like I was on the verge of getting too close to a parked car, Dad would put his hands on top of my own to gently help guide the steering wheel; I loved how they felt—rough and calloused and strong. Later, when I was just about to become a teenager, my father would let me drive all by myself; he would go get some beer, take me to the stadium where the Washington Redskins play football, and sit up under a shady tree while I drove around the parking lot, practicing for the day I'd get my own ride. I'd have to sit on the edge of the leather seat, sticky and hot against my little legs, just to reach the gas pedal and brakes; the truck would jerk violently, making my neck whip as I pushed too suddenly on the gas or got scared and pumped the brakes too hard. Still, I'd giggle every time I passed by my father, who'd be sitting there laughing. "Drive, baby!" he'd yell, and take another swig of his beer. I took my driver's license test in a big-ass lime-green Bonneville without an ounce of fear, because, over the course of years with my father's direction, I'd already mastered driving that pickup truck. I'd already mastered how to control fear rather than let it control me.

That's the thing about fear: Dad had a knack for figuratively knocking it out of you. No one around him was exempt from it—not even adults. Sometime later, long after my parents' own marriage had dissolved, he matured and committed to his second wife. But there was one problem. She didn't have a license and didn't know how to drive. She was too scared. My father wasn't having it. "Let me tell you something. If you gonna be with me, you gonna learn how to drive," he told her. "Fuck that being-scared shit. Come on!" And guess who drives now? He forced everyone he loved to look that devil in the eye and "go tell him he's a liar." Boris Henson lived on that. He wanted me to fear less. To be fearless.

· · ·

My mother was right: I am, in a lot of ways, like my dad. My candor, my humor, my relationship to fear, come directly from him—I carry it deep down in my gut. But while my dad schooled me on the game, it was Mom who taught me how to live it.

Now when I say this to her—when I extend the credit she is due—she shrugs it off, but it is the truth. She stands back and looks in amazement at all that I do: balancing a demanding career with raising my son on my own, and all the while squeezing in some semblance of a personal life. But what I do is not magical, or, in my opinion, unique. All this drive, all this passion, all this get to it and get it done all up in my bones, I get it from my mama. She set up the goalposts and showed me in word and in deed that no matter what lies in the road ahead of me, fear is utterly useless. This she had to do because she was a single mother, heading our family of two in a neighborhood in southeast DC that, when we stepped outside the cocooned paradise she created, replete with my very own room and everything I needed and even some of what I wanted, wasn't the safest place for a woman and her young charge. When she wasn't battling my father, she was battling the streets—literally.

The parking lot was where she did her fighting, or, more appropriately, where she defended herself. It was a trap, really: the parking lot, set in a U-shaped valley between the two large apartment buildings that made up our complex, was always dark, and each entrance was flanked by steps on one side and a laundry room and trash room on the other, neither of which had doors or lights. It was the perfect setup for a thief to knock someone over the head and take all she had, and that's exactly what happened to my mother twice, both times in front of me.

The first time she was robbed, I was six years old. Until that very moment, I hadn't a care in the world. It was late October in 1976, on one of those warm Indian summer nights, and I was floating high, strutting between my mom and my friend from first grade, who, on this rare occasion, had been invited to sleep over at our place. My mother went all out for me, even taking us out for hamburgers and fries at McDonald's, an uncommon treat for us back in those days when money was tight and eating out, even at a fast-food restaurant, was a luxury. Though I was living in one of the most troubled areas of a city in which poverty and hopelessness made neighbor prey on neighbor, I hadn't experienced anything to cause me concern. With my mother, I felt protected, mainly because she always made a way out of no way for me. Because of her, our little family had stability: we never got put out of our place, neither the power nor the water was ever shut off because of an inability to pay the bill, we were never hungry, Christmas was always bomb. I lived for the oversells at Woodward & Lorthrop department store—those exclusive sales when merchandise the store couldn't move was offered to employees for deep discounts. I was fly in high school: Guess jeans on my behind and Coach bags on my shoulders. I still have a beautiful silverware set Mom bought for me when I moved into my first apartment; the only time I pull it out is for special occasions, and when I do, I can't help but think about her and the sacrifices she made to make life beautiful. Knuckles raw, back sore, eyes burning, mind numb, she made it work. Made it so that even in the middle of the hood, where crime ran rampant and there were a lot of folks who had little and lived hard, her daughter found paradise in our little southeast DC apartment. Once I crossed the threshold into the home my mother made for the two of us, I felt like I was arriving at a grand mansion. In her typically selfless form, rather than buy herself a bureau for her clothes or a sofa on which she could relax after a long, hard day's work, she bought me a gorgeous Elizabethan bedroom set, which she outfitted with a Holly Hobbie comforter and a Strawberry Shortcake doll and posters. It was so lavish that for the longest time, I didn't know we lived in the hood or that we were struggling.

On that fateful night of the first robbery, it was to this paradise that my friend and I were going to eat our McDonald's, play dolls, color, and maybe watch a little television, before climbing under the covers to talk and giggle and fight sleep until sleep won out. We were skipping along ahead of my mother in the parking lot, making our way to the main entrance of the building, when all of a sudden, a man wearing a stocking cap over his face ran up behind us. My friend and I were too busy talking and laughing and doing what six-year-olds do when they're excited about a sleepover to understand exactly what was going on. If anything, I was thrown off when my mother giggled, thinking it was a man who was sweet on her, playing a trick. "Oh, George, why don't you stop playing!" she said, laughing, when the man grabbed her.

"Give me your purse, bitch," he snarled, his breath hot on her cheek. The metal of the gun pressed against her temple.

To force her to comply and show her he meant business, he grabbed my mother's hair, jerking her head so hard that she gave a little scream and dropped the fast food and sodas. All three of us froze when the cups crashed to the pavement, splashing liquid at our feet. Terrified, my mother pushed her purse into the thug's hands. "You got any more money on you?" he yelled.

"No," my mother said, shaking.

He ordered us to walk back to the car, and then he took off running. Once she thought it was safe, my mother hurried me and my friend up the stairs and called to a neighbor, who'd come down to empty his trash. He took us to his apartment and called the police, and let us stay with him and his son while the cops asked my mother questions and went looking for the thief. They came up with nothing, which only made my mother more scared. When she searched her pockets for her keys, she found a twenty she'd stuffed there after ordering our food and freaked out even more. "What if he searched me and found out I was lying about not having any more money on me?" she asked. The thought of what he could have done to her or us girls gave her chills. While desperately trying to keep her composure, she arranged to swap cars with her sister and change the locks on our apartment door, seeing as the thief had taken off with everything, including her wallet and the spare keys to our entire life—the apartment, our car, my mom's office. It would be close to an hour before we got back into our place, but the tension was still thick. Though I was only six and barely aware of the mental, emotional, and physical price my mother was paying for the attack, I knew something was wrong, and, even as I played with my friend on the living room floor, I had my eyes locked on my mother, watching her every move. I held my breath, terrified when I saw her reach into her hair, beautiful, long, thick, Farrah Fawcett–feathery and lush, and pull out a clump that the thief had tugged from her scalp. As she dropped her hair onto the table, the tears finally fell. Though on occasion I would see her rub her temples trying to figure out how to pay the bills and the rent so that we weren't put out or left in the dark, this would be the first time I ever saw my mother cry.

We never talked about that moment; my mother wasn't the type of parent who unpacked the gravity of a situation like that for a child's understanding. It happened. Life went on. She soldiered on, and, by extension, because I was her daughter and it was her sole duty to protect, raise, and move in lockstep with me, I did, too. I was scared of the dark for the longest time, but she made me feel safe, and so in my first-grade mind, I was safe. That was the energy she extended to me—the energy she had to employ because my father was not there to offer protection.

Years later, when I was in junior high, it happened again—same parking lot, same apartment building, same circumstances. This time, our city was on the brink of the crack epidemic, and junkies, desperate to score their next high, were out in full force like the zombie apocalypse, preying on anyone within their reach. It was midnight and we were on our way to the car, heading out to pick up a friend whose ride had broken down. Mom always put me in the car first, so I was tucked away in the front seat when a man ran up behind her as she made her way to the driver's side. As she opened her door, the man punched her in the eye—so hard that years later, when she accidentally got hit in the same eye playing softball with her coworkers, her retina tore. "Please," my mother begged the thief as he tugged at the door between them, reaching for her purse, "take my money. Take all of it. Just leave me my purse."

"Shut up, bitch!" he yelled as he wrestled my mother's purse out of her hands and ran off.

I was in the passenger seat, screaming, "No, no, no! Not again!" But my howling was useless. My mother got in the car, closed the door, turned the key, and, without saying a word, started driving in dead silence. She was trying her best to be strong, but with every passing minute, her eye stretched and ballooned and turned various shades of black and blue. In the other unmolested eye, a single tear slowly traced a wet track down her cheek, across her chin, and down her neck.

This was the only home we had. Though she was working her way out of the hole my dad's absence created—she was toiling from sunup to sundown—her salary would take her only so far. It would be perfectly reasonable to think that the two of us, in that moment, in that space in which we'd been violated twice, would be absolutely terrified. Broken. But that's not how it works—at least not for Bernice Gordon. Rather than melt, she once again soldiered on, no doubt because she had no other choice, but I know she also did it because her daughter's life depended on her ability to keep moving, despite the obstacles, despite the adversity, despite what anyone thought about her. She refused to disappear into a cave. She was more cautious, of course; while we lived in that apartment, she made sure from then on that whenever we were leaving or entering the building, someone was around to meet and walk with us. But she never, ever gave me cause to panic. What a profound lesson to learn as I began my own, long journey toward becoming a woman, a lover, a single mother, and a human moving through the world. My mother always said I got all my strength from my father, but I know so much better than that, even if she doesn't realize or refuses to acknowledge it: she taught me, by leading her life, how to be. My father may have put the fire in my heart, but my mother taught it how to beat. They both showed me, by example, how to be fearless.

· · ·

Even today, when I taste fear on my tongue, it's my parents' example I draw on to help me swallow it whole. Nothing could have been truer than when my manager, Vincent Cirrincione, floated the script for *Empire* my way. I was scared to death of Cookie. After all, I'd been trying to escape the typecasting that had come from starring as the loud-mouthed, around-the-way baby mama Yvette, in John Singleton's hit 2001 big-screen hood tale, *Baby Boy*. Yet no matter how hard I tried to climb out of it, I'd been stuck in the muck and mire of screenplays that tried to resurrect that character. The only roles casting directors could see for me were ones that were "edgy" (read: ghetto). Now, after stints on three television shows—one as a police officer in Lifetime's *The Division,* one as a fierce litigator on ABC's *Boston Legal,* one as a detective in CBS's hugely popular *Person of Interest*—an Oscar nod for my role as the adoptive mother of a reverse-aging white child in *The Curious Case of Benjamin Button,* and box office gold in the *Think Like a Man* films, in which I played a businesswoman, I had finally managed to shake myself out of the exclusively stereotypical roles Hollywood producers envisioned for me. I wanted no part of a loud, wisecracking, gaudy ex-con fresh out of prison from a seventeen-year bid on a drug conviction—especially on a television show to which I'd have to commit all of my time. After being locked into fifty-five episodes of *Person of Interest,* going back to the grueling, stifling schedule of television production wasn't even a consideration.

"Leave me alone with this one," I told Vince over the phone during one of the many calls he made, begging me to read the *Empire* script. I'd been back in Los Angeles only for a short while, and I was preparing for a starring role in the play *Above the Fold* at the Pasadena Playhouse, biding my time until another film project came along. "Where's my brilliant film script? I don't care about this mess. I don't want to do it." Vince knew me well—he knew how no-nonsense and in-your-face I could be. He'd learned that the first time I met him, shortly after I moved to Los Angeles and went on a frenzied but exhaustive search for an agent. A friend arranged my meeting with Vince, but he made it clear he wasn't looking for new clients; at the time, he already had a power roster, including Halle Berry, and taking a chance on a young, inexperienced black actress at a time when roles for actresses who looked like me were few and far between wasn't a priority. But I got to him by standing in front of that man and being regular ol' Taraji from southeast DC, with my slightly country drawl and one fingernail painted bright red.

"What's with the fingernail?" he asked.

I looked down at my hand absentmindedly and shrugged. "I forgot to take the paint off," I said matter-of-factly.

After that, Vince launched questions at me in rapid-fire succession, and I answered each of them easily and truthfully, hiding nothing. I told him how I'd studied acting at Howard and got pregnant in my junior year—how I came to Los Angeles with my baby and only seven hundred dollars to my name, but a passion for my craft as wide as the Pacific.

"Where's your son?" he asked when, finally, I took a breath.

"He's with the babysitter."

"So you brought him out here with you?" he asked, surprised. "Usually actors leave the kids with family until they get on their feet in this business."

"No, he's right here with me," I said. "He's where he belongs."

Vince stared at me for a moment, no doubt trying to figure me out. Finally, he ordered me to stand. "Let me take a look at you."

I stood, uncomfortable for the first time in his presence. *What the hell is this, a slave market?* I asked myself as I turned awkwardly. Now I understand that he was simply trying to give me a taste of what it would be like to audition, but I wasn't feeling it in that moment. Annoyed, I snapped at Vince when he began talking again. "What did you say? You're talking too fast. My daddy told me not to trust a person who talks too fast."

Vince smirked. "You're a spunky one, aren't you?" he said. After another beat, he said what I wanted to hear. "Okay, you can do two monologues for me." But, he warned, "you better knock my socks off."

A week later, there I was, standing in his office, reciting for my life. I came prepared with a serious monologue and a funny one, and hit him hard with my presentation, a scene from *Down in the Delta*. When I finished, I'd barely taken a breath before Vince burst into a wide grin.

"I want you," he said. "You were great. You were great, kid. I want you."

I got up the nerve to ask slyly, "So, did I knock your socks off?"

"Yes, you did," Vince said. "That was amazing." Then he let out a hearty laugh as he reached down, unlaced his shoes, and gave me his socks. I still have his olive-green socks somewhere—eighteen years after he agreed to represent me. Ours is a relationship built on trust, mutual admiration, and profound respect, and by now we know each other as well as we know ourselves, meaning Vince knows all the ways to turn my fast no into a slow yes. Which explains why he kept shoving that *Empire* script in my face.

"I'm telling you, you gotta read this one. You'll knock this out of the ballpark," Vince insisted.

"I hate TV. No."

Vince sent me the script anyway, and one night after a fully busy day working on the play, I sat in my living room and picked it up, hoping that reading it would beg off my manager so that he could focus on something else—anything else—instead of Cookie Lyon, the loud-talking matriarch of a record label dynasty. I read the synopsis and sucked my teeth. *Hip-hop? Please. Stupid, corny as hell,* I said to myself as I flipped through the script. Then I got to the page when Cookie first gets out of prison. I was licking my pointer finger to flip through the pages even faster when I got to the part where Cookie's husband, Lucious Lyon, tosses his young, effeminate son in the metal trash can, and I really lost it when Cookie, fresh out of prison, visited her youngest son for the first time, only to end the scene using a broom to beat the hell out of him for calling her a bitch. "What?!" I screamed, alternately excited by the prospects but also wary of its implications: What kind of image is this for black people? How can anybody justify beaming a murdering, thieving, drug-dealing family into the living rooms of a nation grappling with and floundering over race? What would people think of me playing this violent, drug-dealing felon? Will the NAACP come for my neck over this? Though I saw Cookie's heart beating all over the pages, I couldn't see myself playing her.

I called Vince on his cell. "I don't want to do this," I said. "I just don't see the value for me. I've done this before: she's street, she's hood. I don't need to do this again."

"Taraji, just think about it," Vince said. "Can you do that for me? Read it again and think about it."

I promised him I would, and a few days later, I did. As was the case the first time, I was hooked, but instead of my brain judging the characters and calculating how they'd be received by the audience, my gut kicked in: I felt the fear. It wasn't about Cookie or how the television viewers would view her; it was about how they and all the casting directors who'd kept me tucked in that "she's too edgy" box would see *me*. I simply did not want to go back to the bottom of that pool, where the weight of stereotype, judgment, and typecasting could drown my career. Drown me.

It is precisely then that the courage, experience, and trust in myself that my father had ingrained in me empowered me to make the decision to kick fear in the ass. The surest way to do that was to use all that I'd learned along my journey as an actress to figure out how to breathe nuance into Cookie. I understood her. But how would I get everyone else to get her, too?

I decided that, like my father, like my mother, Cookie would be courageous. I would build a backstory for her so airtight, so sympathetic, that viewers and critics alike would see past her troubles and straight to her heart. Think about it: in the real world, people will empathize with the coldest, most calculating evildoer imaginable if he's got a story to tell. A man could be up for the death penalty for killing a dozen children, but if someone gets on the stand and testifies to his backstory—he was raped as a child and tossed in the streets by his no-good parents, in and out of group homes where he was bullied and tortured by kids much worse than him—the jury might be more inclined to give him life in prison instead of the needle. That's how, I decided, I needed to handle Cookie. I created a backstory rooted in courage and her love for her family. It took both—courage and love—for her to deal drugs to make sure her children were fed and the lights stayed on while she supported her husband's dream of becoming a rap star; it took both for her to go to prison for Lucious, rather than have both of them locked up and their babies left out in the street. It is love and courage, too, that makes her want to succeed in her epic battle to wrest control of the family empire from her devious husband: she doesn't want the business for herself; she wants to leave it as a legacy for her sons.

Building that backstory for Cookie helped me really *see* her. It helped me see me, too. Soon enough, I was tossing a middle finger to the notion that playing Cookie would take me right back to that place in my career when casting directors were telling me no because I was too "edgy." *Bitch, please, check your résumé,* I finally said to myself. *Literally, you've done it all except put on a cape, get on a wire, and fly. You got this.*

And I do. I'm not saying I'm invincible. I don't walk around completely fearlessly. Skiing, for example, looks amazing, but I have no intention of climbing into a ski suit, pulling goggles over my eyes, and flinging my body off the side of a mountain. That's a fear I'm not interested in overcoming. Same thing with sky-diving: I will not be jumping out of anyone's airplane and flying headfirst at 120 miles per hour toward the ground with nothing more than a piece of fabric to keep me from crashing into the hard concrete. I'm scared of rodents. And snakes. Don't care for spiders too much, either.

But when it comes to something that stokes my passion, and to things that mean something to me, I tend not to lean on fear. Like my daddy said: fear is a liar. I make a point of calling its bluff.

2

Authentic

I had a mass of thick, tight, kinky curls growing out of my head, and just the thought of my mother pulling that huge, black comb with the wide teeth through my tender tendrils would make me tear up. I couldn't stand hair day. Sundays would roll around and my mother would assemble her tools, her comb, shampoo, towel, the blow dryer, and that big jar of Afro Sheen hair grease, and I would take off running and screaming as if Freddy Krueger's razor fingers were coming for my scalp. Every week, it felt as if a serial killer were pushing me down on a plump pile of pillows atop a set of thick, yellow pages phone books, using her knees like a vise to hold me still while she spent hours shanking my head.

"Shut up all that noise, Taraji," my mother would snap as I shrunk and shrieked under the sharp edge of the comb's tooth, which she used to part my hair into tiny sections that, over the course of hours, she would braid into a mass of fantastic cornrow creations. Sniffling, I'd wipe the tears streaking down my cheeks and just sit there, praying to sweet baby Jesus in the manger, Jehovah, Buddha, Big Bird, and any other deity I thought could hear my cry to give me the strength to make it through.

Still, I'd always manage, as I choked back my tears, to give some kind of direction on how I wanted my hair styled. As early as the first grade, I commanded some agency over my crown and glory, even if it hurt like hell. "Mommy," I'd whimper, "can you make the braids swoop up and to the side so I can wear them in a ponytail with the dark blue beads?" Mommy would oblige the request, no doubt in part to quiet me down, but also because she was intent on extending to me the autonomy I craved.

I was the quirky kid—the one who always had that little extra flair about her. I wanted my hair to be styled a little differently from the rest, my clothes from a store off the beaten path, my shoes a little shinier than the Buster Browns everyone else was rocking—part of my eagerness, early on, to stand out from my peers and be my own, unique, individual person. I'm grateful my mother recognized this early on and agreed to entertain that particular desire of mine—no doubt in part because as a single mother, she really didn't have the time or the inclination to fuss over which way I wore my hair or how many prints and patterns I wore all at one time, though she insisted I be neat, present- able, and respectable. "You're not gonna be out here embarrass- ing me," she always vowed as she smoothed out the wrinkles on my outfits, or chastised me for forgetting to say "yes, ma'am" and "no, sir" when addressed by grown-ups. What's more, she en- couraged my unique style sense and, occasionally, even helped along my peculiar fashion sensibilities. This was true even when I needed new clothes, which we sometimes couldn't afford to buy. It was nothing for my mother, an amateur seamstress who always went to work with her clothes starched to perfection, to whip up a new outfit for me and let me style it in an interesting, fresh way. Countless times, she'd take me by the hand and lead me to the huge file cabinets in our local department store, where there was a treasure of sewing patterns waiting to be mined. I remember one pattern in particular practically calling my first, middle, and last names from that metal drawer.

"What about this one!" I exclaimed, shoving a small envelope with a picture of the outfit I desired into her hand. It was glorious: a three-piece suit featuring a vest with boxy shoulders and pants with decidedly less flare in the hem than what everyone was wearing, plus a matching skirt that skimmed the knee. It looked nothing like the long, lacey, patchwork dresses I saw girls my age wearing, or the painfully corny pullover sweaters and matching pants that were in style back then—the ones that had pictures of Winnie-the-Pooh and all the other popular cartoon characters of the day splayed across the most putrid colors one could conjure up for children's wear. No, this pattern that I'd picked was a standout among standouts—a veritable star that I needed to shine brightly in both my closet and in my fourth-grade class.

"You like that?" my mom asked, taking the envelope into her own hand and holding it up to the light. She nodded her approval. "It is pretty. I have some fabric at the house that's just right for this." She checked the price and, upon determining the pattern met both her budget and approval, marched it to the register, with me skipping behind her, a big, cheesy grin spread across my face as I plotted when I would show off the outfit at school.

It took my mother only about a week to pull together the three pieces with the material she had tucked in her sewing kit: a bundle of maroon, pink, and white plaid jersey knit that she'd found on sale and tucked away months earlier. Every night after work, she would arrive home from her job, prepare dinner, check over my homework, and then hunch her body over the sewing machine. The whir of the needle clicking against the metal of the Singer made her fingers vibrate as she gently guided the material; I'd lie on the floor on my belly, my hands cupping my face, fascinated by the slow, easy dance she did as her foot pushed down on the pedal and she leaned in to the fabric.

Finally, one Monday, my outfit was ready for its school debut. My cornrows were laid, the beads in them clacking. Mommy could throw down on that sewing machine, please believe that; my ensemble fit perfectly, and I couldn't wait to show off her work. I looked *good*.

My mother was in the kitchen, fixing me one of her signature egg sandwiches for breakfast when I rounded the corner out of my room and headed her way. She caught sight of me strutting and beaming out of the corner of her eye, and then turned her full body around to greet me with her warm hug. Her eyebrows, furrowed, betrayed her uneasiness with my style choice. "Taraji, baby, why you got on the vest, the pants, *and* the skirt?"

Ignoring the concerned look on her face, I twirled around with my arms swinging behind me, proud. "Isn't it perfect?" I asked, giggling.

My mother gave herself a verbal pat on the back: "I did sew it up nice," she said. "But I didn't mean for you to wear it all at the same time, baby."

She didn't stop me from going to school like that, though. I wanted to wear every piece at the same damn time, and my mother, ever the encourager, took me by the hand and walked me into my fourth-grade class, kissed me good-bye, and let me swag exactly like I wanted, sending a clear, powerful message that if I liked it, she loved it. I think she dug that her little girl had her own sense of style—that the way I assembled my outfits and fashioned my hair was the easiest and purest expression of my own voice.

. . .

Being your own self—having a voice—was critical in the hood. I came of age at the dawn of the crack epidemic, when a cocktail of societal ills—high crime rates, poverty, drug and alcohol addiction, chronic joblessness, pick your poison—left countless Washington, DC, folks in peril, living on the margins in some of the most vulnerable and dangerous neighborhoods in America. Fighting your way through the pain of that, gasping for air when you're buried to the top of your head in lack with no sign of surplus, can leave you feeling some kind of way. Sometimes helpless. A lot of times hopeless. Like no one gives a good hot damn whether you suffocate to death or you breathe again. Still, even and especially when you feel helpless, it's your ability to be seen and heard that gives you power where you feel like you have none. Even in the darkest places, you exist. Walk through any street in the hood and you'll see what I'm talking about: boys trotting down the sidewalks, their pants sagging defiantly low and their beards and their attitudes thicker and thornier than a rosebush in full bloom; girls with a mass of hot-pink, sea-blue, and fire-engine-red streaks in their hair, nails long, sculpted, and covered in colorful, intricate designs waving animatedly in the air as they get lost in chatter about the day's happenings. Everything about those kids screams, "I'm here, I'm feeling myself, and you're going to *feel* me, too." The respect for that in-your-face style is grudging—it's sometimes even dismissed as tacky. But really, that one black kid doing that weird thing with his pants or his hair is the very definition of trendsetting; the mainstream's first reaction to it is "What in the hell are you wearing?" Years later, it's cool as hell on a Kardashian. Where I come from, we don't need to wait for that validation. As a community, we prize creativity, even and especially if the world we live in isn't quick to reward it. In the hood, having a voice, then, is freedom.

It's also a black thing. Let's keep it real: collectively, we can be a loud, rowdy bunch, particularly and especially among ourselves. I know, this is a stereotype unfairly but typically saddled on the backs of black people; being loud talkers, laughers, and jokesters, dressing flamboyantly and saying exactly what's on your mind when it crosses your mind isn't the sole province of people with brown skin, and race doesn't dictate volume. I've seen my fair share of white, Latino, and Asian folk get loud, too. But get yourself around some black folk when our guard is down and we're around people we care about and our love is filling the space: all bets are off. We can be some loud-ass people.

This was certainly true of my family. We were—and remain to this day—a close-knit crew of trash-talkers: lovers of the put-down, quick with the verbal jab rooted in honesty, love, and a heap of foolery. Whether it was a backyard barbecue at my aunt's house out in the suburbs, or my grandmother's kitchen on the eve of a big Thanksgiving family dinner, or the living room couch in the two-bedroom apartment my mother and I shared, my cousins, aunties, grandmothers, parents, and most everyone else who shared our DNA and our space would have all those within earshot in stitches.

I lived for the annual family summer vacation in Ocean City precisely for this reason. Every year, my father's parents would rent a house in this resort town on the Maryland coast, pile my cousins and me in the back of their ride, and lead the caravan of cars filled with family headed for a week on the beach. Deep into the night, stomachs full with crab cakes and, for the grown-ups, a cocktail or two, there would be fist-bumping and yelling and lots of handclapping to the beat of every syllable in every word uttered, plenty of full-on belly laughs, and furious head nodding, too. From moment to moment, the adults could be alternately arguing and laughing about the efficacy of welfare, the beauty of The Beach Boys' "Good Vibrations," who could get off the coldest put-down in a game of The Dozens, and who always underbid in a raucous game of Spades. No matter the topic, no matter how heated the conversation got, we'd all end the night spent but richer for the experience—happy, with just enough salve to keep our souls right for whatever was to come when we got back home.

Of course, sour language was mixed in; it accentuated the emotion of whatever was being expressed. Like anger ("that bitch had the nerve to look at me like I was in the wrong"), surprise ("what the fuck?"), frustration ("that shit got on my last nerve"), and joy ("you hear how she sang that muthafuckin' note?"). Sometimes, these words just made the joke sound better, or elevated the social commentary. Of course, we kids weren't allowed to say those words, but no one thought twice about saying them in front of us. And I learned from example in which social settings it was okay to curse: in front of family and friends, it was cool, but if mixed company was involved, or if we were in a business setting, offensive language mostly got tucked away.

The one who made himself an exception to that rule? My dad. He was particularly fond of the word "nigga." He called everybody that word. It was his thing—a term of endearment for those he loved and liked, an exclamation point for the ignorant people who tap-danced on his last good nerve, a pronoun that perfectly described pretty much anybody who crossed his path. I was "lil' nigga." His siblings, my mother, my teachers—all niggas. He even called an old white lady "nigga" to her face when she tried to cut him at the grocery store register. "Nigga, you see us standing here on this line, right?" Dad was the king of "no filter," and everybody just rolled with it.

Well, most everybody. I was about age twelve when I learned some serious and much-needed social cues about how my father expressed himself in public settings and the appropriateness of it all. This was around the time that my father, on the mend from being out of work as a metal fabricator, ended up cleaning toilets at the football stadium—the only job he could find. He didn't apologize for that or make excuses; he just took himself to work, collected his check, saved up for a new place so he could move out of his green van, and made the best of his situation, turning all the ugliness that came with his homelessness into something beautiful just for me. My best memories from Dad's job at the stadium were when he'd get tickets and take me to the games.

One game I particularly remember. It was the Cowboys versus the Redskins, the ultimate rivalry. I had on a snowsuit because it was the dead of winter, and I was carrying a sign my dad made for me that he encouraged me to wave to cheer on our beloved home team. I see now how inappropriate it was, a cowboy hat resting on cowboy boots, minus the body that was supposed to be wearing them, and emblazoned on the poster board were these words: THE REDSKINS ARE GOING TO KICK THE SHIT OUT OF THE COWBOYS! I thought our sign was so funny, and it was especially cool that my dad let me march all around the stadium holding it high above my head. I didn't realize it was inappropriate until a fellow fan, some older lady with a prune face and a sour demeanor, turned eight shades of red and literally sucked in her breath loud enough for two stadium rows to hear it above the din of the cheering crowd. "Oh my goodness!" she gasped.

For a brief moment, I lowered that crazy sign, thinking, man, maybe it isn't cool for a twelve-year-old to be carrying a sign with expletives on it. But one look at my dad and I stood firm in my truth: the shit was funny. I waved it like a flag for the rest of the game.

Sometimes, though, my father's candor didn't always feel good or right. My dad had a special knack for digging in the softest spots, and when he did, his tongue left marks. I still wince when I think about that one time when he chastised me in public for having dirty hair. By then, I had wrested full control over my hair styling; my mother put a relaxer in it fairly early on to help ease the detangling process (less pain for me, less work for her), but then handed the job over to me completely when I was about ten years old and fully capable of coaxing my hair into the popular hairstyles of the day. I was washing, blow drying, and pulling my mane into ponytails, yes, but also the little girl version of the Farrah Fawcett, the mushroom, the asymmetrical bobs à la Salt-n-Pepa (you name it, I did it). Eventually I got so nice with the curling irons that I graduated to styling my friends' hair, too—a skill that I would later put to work while in college to make some serious cash doing the 'dos of my fellow classmates who couldn't afford to hit up the professional salon but still wanted their hair styled.

Back when I was doing my own hair in elementary school, I discovered fairly quickly what every black girl knows to be true: the more time between the times I shampooed it, the better the curl would hold. Thick, kinky hair, even in its relaxed state, thrives on the oily buildup that comes when it's not wet, and my hair was no exception, so I'd go two weeks sometimes without washing it. Most times, this wouldn't be that big of a deal. But when it was hot and that Washington, DC, humidity got hold to my head, I did tend to sweat, which would make unwashed hair, full of styling gel, grease, and a bunch of other products, smell a little ripe. A stinky head was not what you wanted around my dad, he of no filters, he who didn't give a damn about hurt feelings. We were on a hot, crowded city bus one day, headed for my school, when my father, who rode with me that day as a treat, humiliated me for having hair that, while curled to perfection, was ripe from having gone almost three weeks without seeing water and shampoo. I was snuggled in his armpit, enjoying the feel of his strong arm around my shoulder, when, his face scrunched, my father sniffed my scalp, put me in a chokehold, and let it whirl: "Why does your scalp smell like goat ass?"

Goat ass.

You have to understand the devastation of having your daddy call you out on a crowded public bus, in the middle of Washington, DC, on a school route through the projects. We were sitting in the back, and my father's voice, loud as if he had a megaphone in hand, filled every empty space between the laughter and noisy chatter among all the Billy Badasses riding to school with us. He said it so loud, I was sure even folks in the two, three cars ahead of the bus heard him. A hush fell over every tongue, all those bubble heads turned, wide eyes searching for the person behind the insult and especially for the target of said slight. I shrunk down as low as I could in that seat, but I couldn't escape the judgment and ridicule from my peers. Everybody was laughing so hard, I was mortified. I tell you this, though: I learned never to go a week without washing my hair.

. . .

My dad didn't let anything slide; he would call anyone on their bullshit—kid, spouse, friend, foe, it didn't matter. I didn't always appreciate my father's voice, but I learned some valuable lessons from him about the importance of speaking my mind, no matter the consequence. If Boris Henson thought you were wrong, he'd tell you about yourself, straight talk, no chaser. That was my father: so real and raw, inappropriate and honest. Isn't that how it should be? Wouldn't you want the people you're dealing with to come from that place? So many people are afraid to live in that space. My father wasn't, though. From that, I learned to never, ever apologize for who I am—to never apologize for my journey. God gave it to me because He knew I could handle it. So much of what I learned from him, I apply to my profession.

My dad is the very essence of my *Empire* character, Cookie Lyon, the drug-selling, truth-telling, time-doing matriarch. Some of my best lines are ad libs drawn directly from the crazy things my father used to say. Give it up to Dad for that classic Cookie commentary about modern-day beauty in *Empire* season one: "You know I was never into wearing all them damn weaves," Cookie snaps. "Girls walking around with their scalps smelling like goat ass."

Beyond the direct quotes, Cookie is like my father in that she is the walking, breathing truth who blurts it out without so much as a fast blink, no matter how embarrassing that truth may be for the human on the receiving end of it. There's a childlike innocence in that. Though the rest of us are trained to stop, think, and manipulate our answers when someone asks a question, Cookie refuses to do such a thing, precisely because of the journey she's taken. She's not just some loudmouth ghetto girl who served time and then came up on some cash; she's so much more complex than that. Cookie's survived seventeen years in a cage and she managed to get on the other side of that prison cell with her soul intact. The system couldn't break her. That's the superwoman power that she has: a voice that matches those gregarious outfits she wears. That is the superman power my father employed when, after losing his home and living out on the streets, he got himself together, found himself a job, and slowly rebuilt his life, finding God, a wife, and second daughter, a new home, and even a studio in which to practice his beloved metalworking. Nothing—no circumstance, no pitfall, no setback—could stop him from acknowledging his struggle and lifting his voice to let everyone know he was always the baddest man in the room, no matter the setback he was processing.

I come by my frankness honestly. I'm an extrovert by nature, and I have no problem being unapologetically bold, loud, foolish, and funny, and saying exactly what's on my mind. I can think of only one stretch of time in my forty-five years when I shrunk around others: when I was in high school. Chalk that up to a bit of timidity around the fellas (and a smidge of developmentally appropriate adolescent angst). When it came to relationships with the opposite sex, I hid. Literally. Under oversized sweatshirts and long skirts that flowed down to my ankles. I didn't want anyone—especially guys—to call attention to how bony and flat chested I was. I weighed one hundred pounds sopping wet, and I looked even thinner than that when I was standing next to my best friend, Tracie (who remains my best friend to this day). Hershey's Special Dark chocolate with an hourglass shape that brought all the boys to the yard, Tracie had the perfect breasts and a round ass. There I was with my little flat chest and a little onion hiding in the folds of all that material I used to wear. The guys were always hot on her; they liked my personality and they thought I was cute, but that was about it. At least that's what I told myself as I cocooned like a caterpillar beneath those baggy outfits. I'm sure now, with the vision and wisdom of a grown woman, that it wasn't so much my skinny frame that kept guys away as it was the energy I was giving off. My lack of confidence when it came to attracting guys made me unapproachable, and so they didn't bother to step to me.

But even as I hid my body, I wasn't afraid to be me. Whether it was singing a song the loudest, making the most noise in a pompom girl competition cheer, or climbing into an ROTC uniform in junior high so that I could show out as part of the drill competition team, I never had a problem looking someone dead in the eye while I gave one thousand. Being "the realest" has its consequences, though. It's one thing for me to pepper magazine interviews with a few curses or talk candidly about my romantic life and the fears I have raising an African American son in front of a roomful of entertainment journalists or on Facebook. It's another thing when standing true affects your work or determines the roles you will even be allowed to audition for. My Washington, DC, accent, colloquialisms, and straight talk, both on-screen and off, have cost me a few roles because casting directors simply couldn't visualize me in the role of the characters I lobbied to portray. I've always been different from Nia Long, Sanaa Lathan, and Gabrielle Union, the actresses who've been the stars of some of the biggest black film classics, like *Boyz n the Hood, Love & Basketball, Love Jones,* and *The Best Man.* I am the sharp, jagged corner to their sleek, smooth lines—always have been, even before I accepted and starred in the role of Yvette, the wisecracking, volatile, thumb-sucking baby mama to the irresponsible hood boy, Jody, in *Baby Boy.*

Every audition would yield notes from casting directors who would write repeatedly, "She's too street," and "She's too edgy," even when I would turn myself inside out to pull off my goofiest, out-of-character best. Once, I flopped, literally, during an audition for a romantic comedy flick I wanted desperately to land. The script was hysterical; I read it and said to myself, *Oh my God, I would kill this.* The scene called for the character to scrape off barnacles from the bottom of a boat, so I ditched my street clothes and showed up to the audition drenched in props: I had flippers on my feet, goggles, a snorkel mask. I jumped feetfirst into that role, figuratively and literally—enough so that the casting directors were able to see my character, rather than me. I got a callback, too, but there was a special request in the notes: leave the props at home. "Too distracting," they said. When I showed up for the second audition, however, the casting directors, it seemed, were distracted by *me*. Scribbled in the second round of audition notes were the words with which they would reject me for the role: "She's too edgy."

That word again.

That's who I became in their eyes—that street girl who talks with that DC twang and is a little loud and "edgy." That's code for "black girl from the hood." For the longest time, Hollywood used my real-life persona to lock me in the proverbial box. All I kept getting from the industry, the profession I adore and in which I've trained, were scripts for baby mamas and ghetto girls. That was true even of films with majority black casts, which sought to appeal to a broader cross section of moviegoers. Eleven years after my first big role in *Baby Boy,* Will Packer of *Think Like a Man,* the hit feature film based on Steve Harvey's *New York Times* bestselling book *Act Like a Lady, Think Like a Man,* initially lobbied hard for me to play Candace, the single mom in love with a mama's boy. When I refused her, they came back and asked me to play Meagan Good's character, Mya, a sexy siren who struggles to forgo sleeping with her love interest for ninety days.

"I want to play Lauren," I insisted. She was the pretty, upscale, savvy woman who let her laundry list of expectations for her significant other—he had to be rich, degreed, in a powerful position, handsome, and this close to perfect—get in the way of love with a struggling chef trying to scare up the money he needed to start his own restaurant. Basically, Lauren was as far away from Yvette as any role could get.

"We're thinking we want a white woman for that role," Will told me candidly.

"Why, in an all-black movie, would you make the most successful character a white woman?" I demanded. "You mean to tell me in this circle of friends, the only very successful person would be a white woman?"

"That's the direction we're going in," Will reasoned. "We think it would be the best route for a diverse cast."

"You know what? Don't call me until you offer me Lauren. I'm not interested in anything else."

I was able to pull that card because I had the pedigree to back it up. But I spoke my mind because my father taught me that there is power in speaking truth to power. That I *had* to do this, and sometimes still do, speaks volumes about Hollywood. After all, I'm a trained character actress. With the right dialect coach, I can give you a London accent, I can give you Becky the Valley Girl all day long. I can pull it back and get corporate when I need to, too. But checks are usually attached to that. I have to get paid to be that person. That is not who I am. Catch me at the grocery store, in the park, at a get-together with my friends, or on my Instagram account, where I dialogue with my loyal fans, and my authentic self will come out. I haven't changed much. I'm still so much like the girl I was in elementary school: confident and connected to my own voice. I can only be Taraji.

3

Drama

Every summer when the sun climbed high, when the blue and hot pinks crept into the mop-head flowers on the hydrangea bushes and the cicadas sang their songs, my mother, her fingers worn to the bone from scratching up the cash and the mental wherewithal she needed to feed, educate, protect, and discipline a kid on her own, would send me down to Scotland Neck, the tiny North Carolina town where her parents raised her and her siblings decades earlier, before they made the journey, one by one, from the Deep South up to my Aunt Janie's house in DC in search of a new life, jobs, and refuge from the drag and degradation of Jim Crow. In the small three-bedroom house, my grandparents, former sharecroppers, lived a simple, country life, and for six weeks out of the year, I would settle in with them, doing what little city kids do in rural towns where the living is easy and the existence is pure: try my best to keep myself from dying of complete and utter boredom.

I would ride in the front seat of my mother's car, kicking and screaming the entire four-hour drive down I-95. Every year, the conversation would be the same. "But all Grandma and Pop Pop do is watch soap operas all day," I'd say, trying to reason with my mother, hoping that my pleas would compel her to turn the car around and head back north. Alas, my fits never worked. My mother would keep right on driving to Grandma's house.

I didn't understand it as a child, but once I had a baby of my own to raise without the help of his father, I understood why my mother would be so relieved when she dropped me off at her parents' house and sped back down the highway: she was about to get a much-needed break from the unrelenting exhaustion and madness of doing it alone. The relief of knowing that while she worked her child was in good hands and safe in her parents' house rather than sitting alone in an apartment in southeast DC, without grown-up supervision or protection, was everything to my mom. She missed me, of course. But for that part of the year, at least, my mom's mind was free and clear.

. . .

Honestly, so was mine. It was in the fields of my grandparents' land, after all, that I found my imagination. There was no Play-Station or Xbox, no Netflix or iPad or any of the other easy distractions today's kids lean on for entertainment. Back then, you had to find your fun, and I was damn good at that. In my hands, a long, pointy stick would turn into an explorer's staff, perfect for pushing back wildflowers and brush in search of worms and lady-bugs; a huge rock would be a dinosaur's toe, stomping through the land in search of pterodactyl eggs to serve at Sunday brunch for my best imaginary girlfriends. I especially loved when dusk fell over the sky; I'd push away from the dinner table, rush out the front door, and fly down the porch steps, chasing after the magical lights bouncing on the booties of the fireflies. I loved how they tickled my palms when I cupped them in my hands; I'd whisper a quick "sorry" to every one of them before I'd squeeze them between my fingers, carefully removing the fluorescent yellow kernel of jelly and adding it to the "diamond" ring and bracelet I'd fashion for whatever evening festivities I'd conjured in my mind. I complained about being cooped up in my grandparents' house with no one but my baby cousins to play with, but quietly I had me a good time.

It was in a tiny pink room there where I found my greatest joy—where I found my desire for stardom. That was my Aunt Glenda's old bedroom. She was long gone from there, but her childhood sleeping quarters remained the same—down to the framed picture of Isaac Hayes in his "Black Moses" getup, the one in which he's rocking some badass dark shades and his bald head is draped in the hood of a long, striped robe—as if frozen in time before she moved out on her own. I'd stare at that picture while I fiddled with the small portable radio sitting next to it; if I turned the dial just so, I could pick up a faint signal from the R&B radio station in Raleigh. If one of my songs was on, I'd crank up that music and tuck myself right in front of the floor-length mirror hanging on the back of the bedroom door, singing into my makeshift microphone fashioned from rolled-up pieces of construction paper, and gyrating my hips as if I were center stage on *Soul Train*. I would get lost in the music, imagining that the little girl smiling and singing hard and staring back at me with those great

big ol' eyes was famous, like Diana Ross, Goldie Hawn, or Lucille Ball. Some days, the hypnotic pull of my own fantasy was so
strong that nothing else in the world existed, not time, not space,
not fireflies or Grandma or even my mother and the friends I was
missing back home.

Falling into my dramatic trances had its setbacks, though,
and it sometimes got me into big trouble, as was the case on one
particular afternoon when I took a break from watching my little cousins Tamera and Cliff to dance in that mirror. My grandmother was in the kitchen, no doubt getting a solid lunch ready
for her grandchildren, and I, the oldest of the bunch at age eight,
was supposed to be babysitting Cliff, who was about four, and
Tamera, who, at almost two, was still in diapers, just learning how
to walk and prone to getting into things. I needed to take a little
break from watching them, though, because Teena Marie's funk
hit "Square Biz" was blasting on that tinny radio, and I wanted
to put on my show in the long mirror. *"I'm talkin' square biz to ya,
babaaaay,"* I sang out from the depths of my gut, completely unaware of the drama that was unfolding just behind me: Tamera
getting out of pocket with a jar of burgundy nail polish. I didn't
catch on until my grandmother rushed in the room and popped
me square on my ass.

"I told you to watch these children, Taraji!" she yelled, wrestling the nail polish from Tamera's hands. "You so busy in here
twisting in that mirror you didn't even see your cousin painting
all over my floor!"

Startled by the hit and the screaming, I spun around, and was
shocked by what I saw. That nail polish was everywhere—all on

the floor, the walls, in the baby's mouth and her hair. I think you can still see a swoosh or two of that burgundy polish in the wood grain on the floor. I was mortified, having been called out for falling down on my duties. For the rest of the day, I felt absolutely horrible and was mildly terrified that something awful would happen to my baby cousin because she drank some of the polish. "I'm sorry, Grandma," was all I could muster. My head was hanging so low. That didn't stop me, however, from singing in that mirror. Best believe I was back at it the next day, this time with one eye on my moves, the other on my cousins.

A few years later, at around age twelve, I would be standing in that mirror again, this time mimicking my idol, Debbie Allen. In my adolescent world, the cast of *Fame*, the hit 1980 movie about the students and faculty at a New York City performing arts high school, were gods. Leroy, Coco, Bruno—I loved them all. When they later adapted the movie into a television series, every week, I would show them my devotion by parking myself in front of the television and clinging to every word they said, every note they sang, every dance move they made, all the drama that defined their big lives at their school. But it was Debbie Allen—she portrayed the dance teacher, Lydia Grant—who, for me, stole the movie with one scene, proving that there is no such thing as a small role. So naturally, when she was on television every week, I'd rush and finish up my homework and any other chores my mother laid out for me so that I could be front and center when the opening sequence flashed across the screen, and then I'd stand there transfixed, waiting to see Debbie with that huge stick in her hand, stalking menacingly around her dance students, sneering her warning in her young charges' faces. Mesmerized, I'd say the lines right along with her: "You want fame? Well fame costs! And right here is where you start paying—in sweat!"

You better believe I wore out that mirror at my grandmother's house that summer, walking in circles with an imaginary stick in my hand, repeating the line with that same signature snarl. (Years later, in a season-two episode of *Empire,* I would pay homage to Debbie by channeling that moment in a scene in which I used a similar stick and attitude to gather together a three-member singing group looking to make a splash on Cookie's burgeoning record label; I hope I inspired some acting hopefuls in the same way that Debbie inspired me.) Unlike my favorite actress at the time, I wasn't saying that line to a bunch of impressionable kids when I was leaning into that mirror as a child; I was inhaling the sentiment for my own inspiration, because by then, I'd caught the acting bug so thoroughly, so completely, that I could not envision myself doing anything else but what my favorite actresses of the time were doing: making the masses laugh, relate, feel something. Entertainers like Carol Burnett and Lucille Ball teleported themselves into my living room every week, pulling out the most ludicrous actions and wittiest words to make me *remember* them. To want to *be* them. I can still feel the workout my abdomen got from the roaring belly laughs Lucille coaxed out of me with that *I Love Lucy* episode in which, at the start of her job at the candy factory, she stuffs her cheeks with chocolate in a desperate attempt to keep up with the conveyor belt of confections whizzing by her. Similarly, I can't shake the look of disgust on Lucy's face in the episode in which she rolls up her pant legs, steps into a barrel of grapes, and feels the fruit squishing between her toes. Watching

Carol Burnett try desperately to smother her laughter in the middle of a funny scene in her variety show gave me an aspiration: to get lost in pretending to be someone else.

This was a skill that I began to hone in an acting class at the Kennedy Center, right around the time Debbie Allen was on the big and small screen, turning me out. My father's older sister, Norma, and my godmother, Brenda, paid for me to go to this particular weekend arts program—in part because they knew I was interested in becoming a performer, but also because my mother had to work weekends and needed a safe place to send me to while she put in her hours. It took a village to get me up on that stage, but only seconds for me to fall in love with everything about being there: the collaboration with my fellow students; the encouragement from the instructors; the excitement of creating stories, memorizing the lines, blocking our places on the sets we created; the smell of and the bigness of the room. I especially craved the attention I got—the applause extended to me when our performances were over. I'd look up and see my entire family, all the way in the back of the room, hooting and hollering my name as I took my bows. They were the perfect audience— egging me on and making me believe that being an actress was really possible. My father was my biggest cheerleader. He would say to me consistently and loudly, like a corner man hyping up a prizefighter in the heat of the ninth round, "Taraji, you already got the glory. You've already collected your Oscar. Right now you're just going through the motions. Stay on your path. You're the greatest actor alive. That's how you walk. Walk in that."

I recognize now how important this was to my development as an actress, even at that tender age. After all, the natural inclination of adults is to devalue the dreams of kids who express an interest in pursuing the arts. Let a kid show any kind of special aptitude for math or science, and the world will move mountains to put him in programs that stimulate his gift. The same goes for children who express even a remote interest in subjects society thinks will lead them toward careers we all tend to consider exceptional: doctor, lawyer, professor, engineer, or if it's the arts, a classical musician and the like. Hardly anyone ever encourages the child who can't sit still, or who runs her mouth a little too much or who lets her imagination soar, to do what is perfectly natural and right to her: consider acting, singing, dancing, or otherwise making a living performing. Even celebrities turn their kids away from the business, though they know firsthand the ins and outs of the trade and could help navigate their children's experience. I get it: the road to Hollywood is littered with the bodies of child stars who couldn't handle the success, money, and fame, people who had quite a time of making the hard transition from child darling to functioning adult. But it seems such a wasted opportunity, so incredibly unjust to steer a kid away from what makes his heart sing.

I thank God that when I was staring at that door to Hollywood, my father and, by extension, my family and some key players in my adolescent and teen years told me I could walk through it if I wanted; in some cases, they even jimmied the door open for me when I thought for sure that I couldn't break the locks. I recognize the importance and especially the beauty in their telling me "You can." This wasn't something anyone told kids from around my way. For all too many, saying you wanted to be an actress was about as realistic as saying you wanted to go to the

NBA, or that you were going to run a Fortune 500 company or be president of the United States. It was a pipe dream. Everyone was too busy hustling to be dreaming, or too scared of what lay outside their zip code to imagine ever having anything more than a stable government job and a couple dollars for the go-go clubs. I was surrounded by friends whose families had to hustle to try to make ends meet in their households, where fathers were absent and mothers were on public assistance, barely feeding the family and hardly scraping by. Jobs were scant, and what was available, mostly, was minimum wage—nothing that could sustain domestic stability, much less support dreams that were bigger than southeast DC. I don't judge the mentality; I understand it and respect that my peers were trying to make a way out of no way in a system that was set up to see them fall hard and fail miserably. Nothing made this more apparent than my junior high school, the Friendship Educational Center.

. . .

Friendship was a school like no other I'd ever been to before. Up until then, I'd gone to a Catholic school where the education was fine, I guess, but the nuns believed in beating ass. One in particular, Sister Theresa with the short hair, big butt, and habit of talking through clenched teeth, was always beating my hands and smacking my butt with rulers and spoons and her bare hands for the smallest of infractions: talking out of turn, moving too slow, breathing. I learned the hard way how to be more restrained. Then, after my mom ran out of money for tuition, I got sent to a halfway decent public elementary school. More changes followed when I was old enough for junior high. Tracking down a decent

school that was educationally superior and safe took a backseat
to my mom's need to have a daughter who was reasonably self-
sufficient. By the time I was headed to the seventh grade, Mom,
who was toiling hard as a manager at a local department store,
Woodward & Lothrop, was depending on me to be able to wake
myself up in the morning, get dressed, eat my breakfast, and hustle to school before the first bell rang—on my own. The school
she enrolled me in was Friendship Educational Center, a junior
high literally across the street from our apartment building.

Hours before my first day there, my mother helped me lay
out my clothes, fixed me my favorite breakfast—I lived for her
scrambled egg sandwiches—and handed me a key to the apartment. It was official: at age thirteen, I joined the ranks of the
neighborhood latchkey kids. We were the children of working
parents, who made very clear that the house key came with very
specific responsibilities and rules: we had to go straight home
after school, lock the door behind us, refrain from bringing over
company, and stay put until a responsible adult got home or risk
getting our behinds beat and everybody else who wasn't supposed
to be in the house unsupervised in major trouble. My mother was
strict like that; she didn't play, and I quickly learned to make a
habit of doing exactly as she said.

I was well prepared for the responsibility that came with taking care of myself in my mother's absence, but I did get into some
trouble along the way. I'm still embarrassed by that one time when
I did have some friends over while my mom was at work and we
called a couple of those 1-900 sex hotline numbers we saw in
some late-night commercials. I didn't know calling those numbers would run up the phone bill; the lady in the ad said the calls

were free. *Free.* What did I know? I was in junior high and trying to impress my friends. We were curious enough about sex at that age to wonder what we'd find on the other side of the line, and we thought calling the number and listening to the women talk dirty in the phone would be fun and funny—nothing more, nothing less. It was, too, until that phone bill came the next month. Four hundred dollars—that was the damage. The look in my mother's eyes when she waved the papers in my face, yelling and screaming and demanding to know what I was thinking, tore my heart to shreds. I knew she was a struggling single mother living paycheck to paycheck, and my thoughtlessness made her cry. I can still hear the disappointment in her voice: "How dare you be so careless? Like, really, how could you do this to me?" she asked. She called the parents of every kid who had been on the phone with me and dimed them to their folks, too. It took quite some time to live that down with them and with my mother.

Ultimately, being home alone wasn't my biggest problem. Friendship was. This school was ghetto; once you walked through the big metal front doors, you could practically feel the hate and broken dreams. We kids sat in this big, brown building with square bulletproof windows so itty-bitty no one could see out of them, in classrooms designed like office cubicles. The classrooms had no doors, paper-thin carpet, and literally *no walls*.

My first day there, I didn't know what to make of either how the school was situated or the wild students that inhabited its space. The kids made quick work of making me, the new girl, feel like I didn't belong. I deserved some of that. After all, within seconds of my arrival, I'd already broken one of the codes: I went to the first day of school dressed up in a new outfit. I had worn floral culottes and a ruffle shirt that stretched up my neck, with a bowtie that matched the print in my pants, plus loafers with shiny pennies tucked in the slots across the top of the shoes. Apparently, I'd missed the memo that said, "Don't be pressed to wear new clothes on day one." More, with my hair curly and pushed to one side of my head, I looked like Laura Ingalls from *Little House on the Prairie*—like an Amish girl who'd just been let out into the world for the first time. My teacher made it that much worse when she made me stand up in front of everybody and introduce myself. "Hi, um, I'm Taraji," I said, nervously fiddling with my bow tie while everybody in the classroom laughed. By the time I slid back into my seat, I was wishing the floor would open up and swallow me and my desk whole. But a quick wave from a girl who'd turned around in her seat to give me a knowing look—one that said, "It's going to be all right and we should totally be friends"—quickly made things better. "I'm Tracie," she mouthed, her introduction coaxing a quick smile from my lips.

From that moment on, it was Tracie and me in Friendship, the worst school ever. Looking back on my time at Friendship now, as a grown woman who put her child through a patchwork of private schools that she handpicked based on how they fit her son's learning style, I can honestly say, "Whoa, that shit was kinda fucked-up." They didn't care about us kids. It was as if they were setting us up to fail. All too many of the teachers were giving a halfhearted effort, the curriculum was substandard, there was no money for books and supplies, noise from the classes spilled over into each other because of the ridiculous design, and no one could get a handle on the student body, half of whom came from homes where crack cocaine had devastated their families. These kids had issues: parents who were addicts, siblings who, caught up in the drug game, were either experiencing or committing violence or being sent to prison for dealing. They were exhausted on both a physical and mental level. Kids were coming to school hungry, confused, angry. Shit was real for them. And they brought all of that to the makeshift classrooms at our school. Honestly, looking back, it resembled juvie hall. Thank goodness I never experienced that for real, but this seemed close to it.

Tracie and I survived it, though, because we were different—we had mothers who held down jobs and worked tirelessly to keep the madness of DC's crack epidemic from crossing our thresholds, and Tracie was lucky, too, to have her father at home. Stability at home translated into the two of us excelling in class (I even made the honor roll), diving headfirst into extracurricular activities like the pom-pom team (Tracie and I were cocaptains), and being noticed by the few teachers who cared about us kids—teachers who could identify and nurture our passions. It also opened the door for both Tracie and me to pursue our passion for acting, even in a school that fell far short in programming that appealed to that particular desire. One teacher in particular, Mrs. Hawkins, saw enough good in Tracie and me that she recruited us to star in a junior high performance of *Macbeth* as part of a competition in a local Shakespeare festival. We played the witches and so thoroughly slayed our performances that we won an award for it—a huge deal considering our school wasn't known for its dramatic pursuits. The recognition, and Mrs. Hawkins's belief in us, only pushed Tracie and me to hunt for more opportunities to show off and show out. One summer, I even put all that dancing I'd done in front of the mirror back at my grandmother's house in

North Carolina to good use: Tracie and I performed DeBarge's hit single "I Like It" in the school fashion show, and I hit that high note El DeBarge rides the song out on like there was nobody else watching—like the world consisted of only me, the stage, and that microphone. We killed it, and we were thirsty for more.

So good were our grades and our extracurricular accomplishments that by the end of eighth grade, both Tracie and I were invited to the math and science program for advanced students, a curriculum that would take us out of that godawful junior high school and place us in a specialized series of courses at our local high school. It turns out, though, I wasn't ready for the transition. Maybe I was too young to be around all those high school students, or perhaps it was simply developmentally appropriate for me to act the donkey at that age, but when I got to Ballou High School, I was the good girl gone bad. I laid all my nerdy ways to the wayside, dumbed myself down, stepped away from acting, and quickly established myself as the class clown. I was still creative, but now it was in much more distracting, destructive ways, which helped me fit in with the rest of the student body at Ballou, a school in which a creative child like me did not belong. One teacher, Mrs. Esther, kept me from going off the deep end. She could have easily failed me in her English class, but instead, she'd laugh at my disruptive ways and embrace all my drama. Even when my mother sat in front of her in those little chairs for the parent-teacher conferences, Mrs. Esther had my back. That first meeting, I was sitting wide-eyed and nervous next to my mother, imagining all the terrible, painful ways she would put me in my grave for all the trouble I caused in English, when Mrs. Esther made clear she wasn't interested in diming me. Rather than talk bad about me or tell the exact truth, she protected me. "You know," she said, slowly, shifting her eyes in my direction then back at my mom, "she's a talkative child. She talks a lot." What she should have been saying was, "Look, your daughter is bad as shit. She comes to class late and when she gets here, she's disruptive. She stands up and she blows her nose like a go-go band trumpet, and when I lock her out, she tries to heave-ho her way through the door. By the time she's finished acting the clown, twenty solid minutes of instruction are wasted."

She let me get away with that kind of behavior because she knew it came not from dire circumstances at home, but a lack of a creative outlet for my true passion. Rather than turn me in, she tried to turn me back on to acting, suggesting that Tracie and I compete in the local Hal Jackson's Talented Teens competition, a popular pageant for girls that focused not only on beauty and comportment, but also, and most significantly, talent. I jumped at the opportunity, if only for the chance to stand up in front of an audience and show off my skills.

· · ·

For weeks, Tracie and I worked on our monologues—dramatic scenes we created on our own and rehearsed together after school. I settled on a story about a young girl struggling with her identity: my main character was unpopular, unattractive, sexually abused, hated by her mother, ridiculed by her peers—a tragic, not-so-sophisticated precursor to *Precious,* the character created by Sapphire and brought to life in the Lee Daniels 2009 drama starring Gabourey Sidibe as a Harlem teen mom of two who, after escaping horrific incest and abuse at the hands of her parents, winds up HIV positive. All the other contestants went on that stage tap-dancing or playing their flutes and singing their happy songs, but I was going for drama. I wanted my monologue to be so moving and fierce and memorable that when I finished performing it, Hal Jackson himself would take me by my hand and introduce me around Hollywood as the next Oscar-winning star.

My biggest supporter was, of course, my dad. Though he was only just getting back on his own feet after scoring a modest-paying government gig, he found the time to drive me back and forth to rehearsals and even took me to buy my dress, a lovely, pastel-colored number we both agreed would make me stand out among the other contestants. "Oh my God, this is the sweetest thing ever!" the salesgirls exclaimed when my daddy walked through that storefront holding my hand, talking about "My baby's going to be in a pageant. Make her look pretty."

The night of the pageant, I wasn't nervous at all. I flaunted the gown Daddy bought me in front of the judges. And when the announcer called my name for the talent contest, I walked from behind that curtain and traversed the stage to that microphone, with the spotlight shining in my eyes, and I performed the monologue I penned as though the very oxygen I breathed depended on its impact. I raised my voice when the moment suited it, and whispered when I was searching for a more quiet, meaningful response from the audience. They were with me, too—I could feel the energy in the room. It was like a high. All eyes were on me, clinging to my every word. And then, I went in for the kill: I walked over to an imaginary window, said my final line, and twirled my body to the ground. As I lay there, my body splayed awkwardly across the floor and my eyes shut tight, the heaviness of the scene fell like a pall over the audience. It took them a beat to realize my character had committed suicide. Finally, a collective gasp rose in the air.

And then, silence.

After a lot of murmuring, I heard someone pounding his palms together, clapping furiously. "Yeah, baby!" my father was yelling from his seat in the middle of the theater. "That's the way you do it! That was beautiful!"

It was like that moment in Eddie Murphy's *Coming to America* when the singer Randy Watson, portrayed by Eddie, finishes croaking his tragically inept Las Vegas–style version of George Benson's "Greatest Love of All," then tries to bolster the audience's weak applause by tossing the mic on the ground, stomping his feet, and yelling, "Sexual chocolate! Sexual! Chocolate!" My father meant well; he was going to support his baby to the end, even if the audience didn't quite embrace the drama and suspense I brought to my piece. But damn, it was awkward.

I didn't win that night; I was a runner-up to Tracie, who ended up representing Washington, DC, in the national finals of the competition in California. She came in second there, but returned to our hometown having been thoroughly turned out by the glamour of Hollywood. "This is it, Taraji," she said breathlessly when, finally, we were able to talk. "We have to get out of Ballou and go to Duke Ellington. That's where we belong."

· · ·

I wish I could say that being admitted to the prestigious Duke Ellington School of the Arts, alma mater of such luminaries as the comedian Dave Chappelle, the opera singer Denyce Graves, and the actors Clifton Powell and Lamman Rucker, was as easy as saying, "Let's go to school there," but it wasn't. There was an inter-view process and an audition, and while Tracie managed to secure a spot with her Hal Jackson competition monologue, mine, again, fell flat. I didn't get accepted, and I was devastated—convinced that I simply didn't have what it takes to be a star. I held on to that no-tion, too, giving up acting altogether, not just at Ballou, but later also at Oxon Hill High School, where I transferred after my mother moved our family across the DC border into a newer complex in Maryland. So shook was I by the loss that, though acting was still a passion of mine, I shelved the desire and focused instead on other things: fashion shows, sewing, even science and math after I took an educational detour into a science program at the University of the District of Columbia, where I learned how to solder electrical boards and build motion-sensor lights, transistor radios, and even a robot. I really liked the soldering part because it reminded me of what I'd seen my father do when he'd taken me along on a few of his jobs, installing wrought iron doors and windows on these huge houses out in the suburbs. I loved putting together the circuit boards in particular because it was like assembling a puzzle: you had your circuits, your LED, your conductors, and your energy, and you soldered it all together and it worked—easy. Somehow, in my brain, that translated into *Yes, absolutely, you could do this for a living!* I was so thoroughly sure that acting wasn't in my cards that when it came time to apply for college, I chose to go to the Greens-boro, North Carolina–based historically black college North Car-olina A&T to study—get this—electrical engineering.

Engineering.

I knew better. Truly I did. It took not much more than a se-mester and a grip of failed math tests for me to face that fact and come clean to myself: *You're not a mathematician. This is not where you're supposed to be.* I'd fail precalculus on one side of the campus and then, in a different building on the other side of the property, I'd get A's writing monologues, dressing up in character, and performing my pieces in English classes. There was no fighting the gravitational pull of acting. Everything about me—the way I dressed, the way I expressed myself, the way I used my left brain instead of my right—betrayed my true desire to act. Sized up next to the kids in the sciences, I most certainly didn't look like anybody's mathematician. I fashioned my hair into a loose top-knot that fanned out across the crown of my head, and cropped my pants and bedazzled them with oversized, glittery buttons. "Girl, what you got on?" the geeks would ask, trying to make fun. But I didn't care. It didn't matter if I were wearing a tin man outfit, I was totally committed to being eclectic—different. Much more like the kids over in the English department—my tribe.

In other words, I was the circle trying to fit into the square peg. A girlfriend of mine from high school who went to North Carolina A&T and saw one of my class performances would tell me years later that everyone at our school knew I was in the wrong place. "I looked at you," Candace said, "and I thought, *She doesn't belong here. She needs to be acting.*"

It was my father who gave me the air I needed to fly out of the math department in North Carolina and into the theater department at Howard University, the prestigious historically black Washington, DC, school that boasts a roster of successful alumni who've gone on to make indelible marks in politics, the sciences, media, and, most notably for my purposes, the arts. I grew up practically in Howard's backyard and had long admired the huge list of Hollywood stars who honed their craft in the classrooms of the university, including Ossie Davis, Debbie Allen, Phylicia Rashad, and so many others. All it took was one conversation with my dad to take a fresh look at studying there.

"I failed, Dad," I told him over the phone after getting yet another F in math class. "I've never failed anything in my life."

"Good," he said simply.

"What do you mean, 'good'?" I snapped. "I can't afford these failing grades."

My father was uncharacteristically quiet; he was thinking up just the right combination of words to make it plain. "You had to fall on your face to see that's not what you were supposed to be doing," he said finally. "Now get your ass back up to DC and enroll in Howard's drama department. Do what you're supposed to be doing." As was my custom, I took his advice.

In other words, I was born for this. Built for it. I may not have that Oscar my father claimed for me all those years ago, but he was right: every move I've made since those days gyrating in my grandmother's mirror came in divine order to bring me to this moment, to my dream of being an actress. If my father were alive today, he would call it like he saw it. "I told you, lil' nigga. I knew you were going to be a star."

4

Hustler

All my life, I've been a hustler. Where I come from, that's what you did when you wanted that fresh pair of sneakers, or the gold necklace that spelled your name out in bubble-letter script, or that pack of cherry Now and Later candy your mother didn't want to blow good money on, because every penny she wasted on crap you didn't need meant not having the cash for the things that mattered: the light bill, gas for the car, food for the refrigerator, rent so you had a place to lay your head at night. Of course, there were plenty of kids around my way who hustled in the traditional sense of the word to get what their families couldn't afford; there are back alleys and dark shadows all throughout southeast DC that tell that story. But my hustle wasn't nearly as sinister or desperate. I was just really good at relieving the people around me of their cash so I could have a few dollars for my pocket—a skill I was practicing as early as eight years old back in 1978. If the lady down the hallway with all the kids had to run to the Safeway to pick up some eggs, cereal, and milk, I'd step right in. "Go ahead, I'll watch the kids . . . for five dollars." Somebody needed help getting bags up the stairs? I'd chip in for a dollar or two. Nobody had to worry about sweeping a porch, folding laundry, or corn-rowing their daughter's full head of hair while I was around: for a fee, I'd handle all that and toss in a smile, free of charge.

I brought that "get money" spirit with me everywhere I went because there was little money to spare in my house. I saw my single mother struggling to make ends meet on her salary from Woodward & Lothrop department store (back then, it was known as Woodies); she may have risen from the stockroom as a price tag attacher to her own office as divisional manager of distribu-tion and logistics over the course of my childhood, but she was still raising a kid on her own in one of the most expensive cities in America, without any financial help from my father.

With a baby on her hip and not so much as a pot to pee in or a window to throw it out of once she left my dad, my mother moved herself first into my father's sisters' house in northeast Washing-ton, DC—the home my aunts Norma and Brenda inherited from my father's parents after they moved to North Carolina—and then, later, into the nearby basement of my mom's oldest brother, Buck, until she could save up enough money to get on her feet. Her family, firmly planted in the upper-middle class, was gener-ous like that—always stepping in to help support us. Buck lived in a two-bedroom row-house duplex with his wife, Joyce, and their four children. The two boys shared one room, I shared a second bedroom with the oldest daughter, and the baby girl slept with her parents, while my mom made a home in the basement, sleeping on my twin-sized bed, the only furniture my dad would allow my mom to take from our apartment when she left him. My uncle didn't charge my mom rent; all he wanted was for her to help with the utilities. That's how close, loving, and caring my mom's family was and still is, even more so today.

Still, becoming self-sufficient enough to find her own place was an uphill climb for my mother; securing a deposit, first and last month's rent, and moving fees on a not-so-generous department store salary was no easy feat. And just when she thought she was getting somewhere, a pipe burst and flooded my uncle's basement, water seeping into all of my mother's treasured possessions; her furniture and clothes, which she always kept so pristine, now soggy and reeking of mildew, were completely ruined. She ended up moving upstairs and sleeping on the sofa, with the eight of us cooped up in that duplex for months. I know this much, though—I was so happy to be there because spending that much time with my cousins was like having siblings. Later, more havoc rained down on her belongings: my uncle's damn dog chewed through her business shirts. At one point, she was so broke she couldn't afford even to buy herself a pair of dress shoes; she wore the one pair she had to her job every day for an entire year.

Eventually, we moved into a garden-style apartment on Livingston Road, in southeast DC, right on the border of Oxon Hill, Maryland. My mom scratched and saved every penny she could and cashed in some savings bonds she'd been keeping for me to pay the first and second months' rent plus the security deposit. When we moved in, we had nothing but that twin bedroom set my father let my mom take and the few clothes we had left after the flood. Both by mom and I slept on that twin bed until she woke up one too many times to find me lying on the floor. My Aunt Pat and her husband, Uncle Casper, gave my mom an extra full-size bed frame they had stored away, and my mom got herself credit approval for a mattress set that cost her $188. I don't know how she can still remember that exact amount, but I'm guessing when you live through hard times and make it out, those things are forever embedded in your memory. Gradually, mom was able to purchase a used kitchen table and two chairs from Salvation Army and a living room set from a used furniture store nearby.

Though she tried not to show it, living paycheck to paycheck got to her. It would show up on her face, mostly in the evenings when she'd sit at the kitchen table, hunched over a stack of bills, rubbing her temples and fighting back the tears when she'd see the words "Final Notice" and "Past Due" written in bright-red block letters at the top of her statements. I may have been too young to process the gravity of it all, but I was intuitive. My mother was hurting. I remember once when I was eleven years old, tiptoeing up to her in my pajamas and running my hand over her back. "Don't cry about money, Mommy," I implored her. "I'mma be rich one day."

She just kept on keeping on, as they say. An excellent provider, she made sure I always had what I needed, and occasionally what I wanted, too. Still, I knew something as simple as a trip to Burger King or as extravagant as a fancy purse meant that she would have to go without something else, sometimes the basics. It was also made clear that when I was of age, there would be no sitting on my ass being lazy while my mother busted her behind at the department store. When I was too old for summer visits with my grandparents, when the late seventies gave way to the mid-eighties, I stayed in DC and worked, first with the Marion Barry Summer Youth Employment Program when I was fourteen and fifteen, and then, when I was old enough for a work permit, in sales at Woodies. My mother was teaching me early on that if I really wanted something, I better be prepared to hustle hard to get it on my own.

Nothing could have been truer when it came time to get that college tuition together for Howard University. I'd gone to North Carolina A&T in part on the wings of a grant from a local youth-services organization. But the university was holding my transcripts hostage until I paid off the balance of what I owed for my year there. When I got back to DC, I had to hit hustle-hard mode to make the transfer. First order of business was to quickly nail down a gig and a place to stay, as by then my mother had moved to the suburbs with my cousin to cut back on expenses. I ended up moving into the basement of the house owned by my stepmom and father, who by then was on his way to getting himself together with a steady job of his own, plus a wife and my little sister and stepbrother to support. Once I was settled, I got a job at the Pentagon, paid off my debt to North Carolina A&T, and got down to the business of classes at Howard.

Still, I was restless and headstrong, two characteristics that certainly go hand in hand with being a hustler. If your game is tight, you get what you want, but once you do, you're automatically on the hunt for something bigger, something better. My want once I got into Howard and got myself a couple of dollars was more independence. Asking my parents for rides back and forth to school, and coming home to find my nosy father rifling through my things, was more than I could handle. I'd fume and pace from wall to wall, whisper yelling and shaking my fist at the ceiling: "Why are you in the basement, in my space? Nothing down here concerns you!" Then I'd stomp away. "I'm twenty! Stay upstairs with Shawn and April. That's whose stuff you need to be going through, not mine!"

I couldn't get out of their house fast enough, and as soon as I amassed a critical amount of cash, I scored my first car in 1990—a used Nissan Pulsar, crisp white with a T-top. My mother's sister's husband, Uncle Jessie, sold it to me for six thousand dollars. You couldn't tell me nothing. I drove straight from his house to Duke Ellington High School to surprise my best friend, Tracie, who worked there. The sun was high, my radio was bumping, and I was beeping the horn when she walked out. "Girl, it's me!" I yelled, waving wildly and smiling so hard you could see my back teeth.

"Oh my God!" Tracie yelled as she took off running toward me. I jumped out of the car and posed on the hood like I was a star on the cover of *Essence;* Tracie ran her hand across the side panel as if she were fingering the finest silk. The two of us went completely nuts on adrenaline and excitement. On the weekends and during the summer when I wasn't working, the only thing my parents saw of me was the taillight of my Pulsar. Tracie and I were either laid out on the beach in Ocean City, or running up I-95 to New York to see what we could get into there.

This had my mother feeling some kind of way because for so long, it'd been her and me. Now, with my newfound independence, she sensed that I was growing up—that I was pulling away from her control and making some decisions on my own. She was also upset because though I thought I was grown, I was still a twentysomething dumbass whose irresponsible ways were costing me some serious cash. My car, for instance, was an incredible money suck. More often than not, the car was booted by the city for some parking violation. I knew that street cleaning rules dictated I get my ass out of bed and move my car from one side of the street to the other, but if I'd drunk too much the night before, dragging myself out from under the covers wasn't a viable option, so the Pulsar would take the hit: a boot on the wheel until payday, when I could scrape together enough cash to pay the ticket and have it removed. Some days when I didn't have the money, I'd have to walk right past my car on the way to school, trying real hard not to look at that big yellow hunk of metal clipped to my wheel. The feeling was even worse on days when I was running late and my mother had to drive me to campus. Real talk: you're not winning if you insist you're grown but you're looking at a boot on your ride from the front seat of your mom's car.

. . .

That pile of tickets didn't stop me from wanting more independence, and hustling harder to get it, though. I had my eyes on moving out of my father's basement, and my little Pentagon check wasn't cutting it, what with all the tickets and the debt I'd run up on my credit cards. Clothes. Gas for the Pulsar. Eating out. Renting hotel rooms in Ocean City, where I'd spend the weekends. More clothes. Spending all my money on ripping and running up and down the highway and trying to look good doing it. Soon enough, my balances crept so far north that keeping up with even the minimum payments was out of reach. Talk about

Oscar-worthy performances? The bill collectors who called my house got the best of my earliest ones. *"¿Qué?"* I'd yell into the receiver, putting on my best Spanish accent to throw off the collectors who blew up my phone looking for their payments. "Taraji no live here!" This would hold them off for a little while, but really what I needed to both keep up with my bills and get out of my father's house was a solid hustle, something bigger than that desk job with the government.

That's when Taraji's Basement Apartment Salon opened its doors to my fellow friends, cousins, aunts, fly girls at Howard, and whoever else had money, and I began hooking up wet sets and acrylic nails for extra cash. Twenty dollars could get you looking right for Saturday night; another twenty could get you a full set of acrylic nails, which would have cost double that in one of the local salons. I was good at it, too; so good, in fact, that had this acting thing not worked out, I'm sure I would have been someone's cosmetologist somewhere, styling hair, doing makeup, and hooking up nails.

When I wasn't supplying everyone's beauty needs, I was talking drunk diners out of tips as a singing waitress on the *Spirit of Washington,* a dinner barge that floated down the Potomac River. I made a killing singing my signature song, Tina Turner's "Proud Mary." I'd start the song on a slow simmer, just like Tina, swaying to that deep bass while I worked over those "rolling on a river" lyrics. With every note, I could see the diners, swaying and leaning forward in their seats, just waiting, practically holding their breath for that explosive moment when the horns blared and I'd take off spinning, leaning into the mic and practically growling Tina's song, with the National Harbor, the Capitol dome, and the Washington Monument twinkling in the distance. It was a great job for an artsy person with an outgoing personality and a thirst for the spotlight and an easy dollar. On a typical night, I pulled in one hundred dollars—a lot of money for a college student. Certainly enough to move out of my father's basement and into my own apartment. The guests liked my voice just fine, but it was my swagger that got me paid: I could pour wine and, more important, connect with people.

I was from the hood, but I wasn't hood. On the weekdays I was with "Man-Man," "Peaches," "June Bug," and them, but on the weekends, my mother had me out at my cousin Kim's house in Waldorf, Maryland, where all the white folk lived before gentrification turned "PG County" into "The County" and "Maryland" into "Murland." There I hung out with Becky, Mary Sue, Josh, and Brock, and picked up how they moved and thought and talked to one another. In the summertime, I'd shift yet again. I would head down south to the sticks of rural North Carolina to live with Grandmaw and my family. Those experiences with all different kinds of people in all different kinds of places ultimately helped me become comfortable with all people. Like a chameleon, I learned to blend in with my environment. It's that gift, coupled with a strong work ethic and absolutely zero fear of working hard, that's given me quite an advantage when it counts as an actress.

Yet hustling isn't always about making the most money or gaming the system; in my profession, it's about putting in the work and perfecting the craft. This, I learned on the stages of the Howard University Department of Theatre Arts, where the very finest instructors turned out some of the most respected, prolific working actors ever captured on television and film. There was Ossie Davis, Lynn Whitfield, Roxie Roker, the cinematographer and director Ernest Dickerson, and the Allen sisters, Debbie and Phylicia Rashad, building a legacy, and a new generation of performers like Isaiah Washington, Wendy Raquel Robinson, Anthony Anderson, Marlon Wayans, Paula Jai Parker, and Carl Anthony Payne Jr., whose light shined a path, showing those of us who came directly after them that having a career was possible. But I never would have made it without the direction of the professors, who drilled into every one of us that it wasn't enough to simply show up. They knew this because they, too, were working actors. Al Freeman, Jr., the head of the fine arts department when I was there, was an Emmy Award–winning television and movie star who had not only enjoyed a long career on the soap opera *One Life to Live,* but also had been in movies as far back as 1960 and even starred as Elijah Muhammad in Spike Lee's *Malcolm X* while chairing Howard's drama department. You didn't show up for class wasting his time. Another professor, Fran Dorn, was the queen of Shakespearian theater in DC, and she was on a couple of television shows to boot. You didn't show up to her class to waste her time, either. Schooling us on how to bring it to the stage wasn't about the check for them; they were at Howard because one, they cared about the craft, and two, because they wanted the people coming behind them to carry the torch high. If you didn't? They would put your ass out. They didn't care if you were cute, if you had long hair, pretty skin, if you were mixed and lighter than a paper bag, if you came from a family that could afford a maid and a chef or from a home where ramen noodles were considered fine cuisine. The only thing that mattered was your answer to these questions: "Can you fill this space with the truth of this character?" "Can you build a beautiful set?" "Can you style the most incredible hair to look exactly like it would have looked in this or that era?" "Can you do the best makeup?" "Can you get these props organized and on the stage when they need to be there?" If the answer was no, don't even look at the stage. The kids who were up there? They earned that.

I hustled my way onto that stage. I showed up to my first classes at Howard in the fall of 1990 just as the campus—a jewel-like oasis in the middle of bustling DC—started buzzing about Professor Mike Malone's annual student production, this one of the hit Broadway play *Dreamgirls,* about the trials, tribulations, and triumphs of a trio of soul singers who become international pop stars. If you were a theater major, you wanted to be in this play, because already, even then, it was a classic in the making. Plus, you could earn money by being in a Mike Malone production, as his works were consistently picked up by the Kennedy Center, which paid the actors and production team for the performances—a great way to build your résumé plus put some change in your pockets. Because I could not transfer in until I had paid my outstanding balance at A&T in North Carolina, I arrived after the semester started, completely clueless about the auditioning process and too green to try anyway—still convinced that though my audition got me into Howard's doors, I wasn't ready for a part. Still, I wanted to be there; first of all, my bestie, Tracie, was playing Deena Jones, the singer whose relationship with the group's manager leads to her epic rise over her fellow bandmates. Plus, watching her and my fellow classmates rehearse was mesmerizing. I wanted in on that action. I quickly signed up to work in the props department, which not only afforded me class credit for one of my theater department electives, but also put me in the room for all the rehearsals.

I took full advantage of my time there, too, laughing with the cast members, all the while doing my job and being as helpful as I could be, even at weekend rehearsals, which I wasn't required to attend. Soon enough, I became friends with everyone, from the principal actors down to the chorus and musicians, and even caught Mike Malone's attention, so much so that he couldn't help but see me when he was looking to fill minor roles in the chorus or as onstage extras. He would announce another part and there I would be, front and center, letting out a loud cough to call attention to myself, signaling that he should pick me, the props girl who was eager for a shot onstage rather than behind it. Professor Malone didn't pay me any mind at first; I was but a nuisance, every bit as distracting as an annoying fly. But I was funny. One afternoon, when he announced to the chorus that he needed someone to make a simple cross from stage right to stage left in a transitional scene, I made him feel my presence.

"Okay, listen up, people," he said, standing on the stage, fiddling with pages, marking off something with his pen as the cast stood around, waiting for direction. The room fell silent. "I need someone to make a stage cross."

At just the right moment, I let out, once again, one of my signature coughs—a sound that I'd been making at every rehearsal that I didn't even need to be in; it was so loud, the entire room burst into hysterics, again.

Malone looked in my direction and narrowed his eyes into slits. I stared right back at him, my round eyes as big as saucers, silently pleading with him for my lucky break. Finally, he shook his head and let out a sigh. "All right, girl, get your ass up here and we'll see what you can do."

I will say this: my role was as basic and minor as a role could get—so much so that we barely rehearsed it. Hell, it wasn't even a role. All I had to do was walk across the stage. But you couldn't tell me I wasn't about to be *the* star of that stage. There was nothing in the script for this cross. But remember: I had already learned from Debbie Allen that there is no such thing as a small role. So I carped that damn diem. I created a character for the cross: I made myself a seamstress delivering Deena a potential show dress. So the excitement I exuded crossing from stage right to stage left could be seen and felt. Because I also had to cross back stage left to stage right, I decided to make that moment about being totally rejected by the diva Deena. And believe me, when I say all of that studying of Carol Burnett and Lucille Ball kicked in? It made my small but impactful role, which wasn't even supposed to be a scene, one to remember.

Nothing in the script gave a description of this seamstress or her motivation beyond the fact that the dress she picks for Deena is rejected, but I spent countless hours considering that seamstress's motivation nonetheless. What expression would she have while presenting the gown to Deena? How would she walk on the way to Deena? How would she slink away after the rejection? All of it. I even dreamed up her costume: little framed glasses, stockings under a frumpy dress with slouchy knee-high socks, a zaniness about the colors. She was nobody to everybody, but I made her somebody to me.

When opening night came, I was ready. My heart was beating

so fast on the side of that stage waiting for my part, I'm surprised I didn't pass out. Finally, Deena said the line that gave me my queue. I sashayed across that stage with a gown I thought was the most beautiful dress in the world, matched only by my wide, beaming grin. Everything about my body language said, "Yes, Deena, of course you will choose my dress for your world tour."

Deena, unimpressed, opened the garment bag and angrily tossed it back at me, throwing in a few choice words for good measure and telling me to get the hell out of her sight. Devastated but convinced I'd been wronged, I stomped back across the stage, stopped midway, tossed a nasty side-eye at Deena, and then stomped out the door without saying a word.

I was on the other side of the curtain, giggling with nervous laughter, floating with excitement when my ears were finally able to focus on the audience's reaction: they were hysterical with laughter. Out of everything that was happening onstage, it was my timing and foolery that they remembered—a moment that came at the end of a transition scene. I may have had a bit part, but I was *in Dreamgirls,* and folk who counted were paying attention, including my mother. She wasn't convinced there was a career in acting, and having scrimped and saved to get three steps forward only to consistently fall two steps behind, she wanted something more secure for me than "starving artist." That's all she could see for me, her child who was born with neither silver spoon nor serious connection to Hollywood, a glittery mirage seemingly so far from reach it might as well have been on the other side of the galaxy. Her questions made sense: "I'm a single mom, how on earth can I support you in this? What if you can't get a job? Then what?" It was hard to argue against her judgment. But on the opening night of *Dreamgirls,* when she watched me strutting across that stage, finally she *saw me,* and she pledged her unconditional support.

When I wasn't working on my role, I was still prop mistress, but I continued studying everyone else's roles, too; I knew every line, every song, every stage direction, where every prop lay. When a fellow student with a key role as a singer in the opening of the play had to drop out, I was ready. Professor Malone took to the stage to announce her part was open, and I jumped at the chance to play it.

"I got it! I can do it!" I shouted, raising my hand like some nerd eager to answer the teacher's question.

Professor Malone shook his head, looked me up and down, and smirked. "Well, you better get your heels and come in here tomorrow ready to show me what you got."

"I have my heels right here!" I said, reaching down into my knapsack.

"All right, then get your ass up here and sing the song," he said.

I hurriedly slipped on my shoes and took my position as the music director counted down, and when he got to "one," I hit every last one of the steps and notes with a jubilance that made the entire cast cheer me on. When, finally, they all quieted, I looked over at Professor Malone, eager to hear the magical words. "Well," he said, "I guess you got the part."

The next thing I knew, the show was such a hit, it was selling out every night, with fans from near and far coming to see the wonder that was the Howard University Theatre's *Dreamgirls* production. So successful was the first run that Professor Malone revived it for a second run the next academic year, catching the attention of a major theater producer from Hong Kong who happened to be in DC. That producer loved the play so much that he paid for our entire production—the actors, the directors, the wardrobe, the props, everything—to fly to Hong Kong for a two-week run, which, too, quickly sold out, upstaging even a professional production of *42nd Street*. Fans were showing up to our fancy hotel, waiting in the lobby to get our autographs and take pictures with the cast. It was surreal—until then, except for summers down south with my family, I'd never been out of the country, but there I was, living out loud every fantasy I'd ever had of traveling the world as an actress. "Shoot, I'm on the right page," I said, hugging myself as I gazed out the window overlooking the hills of Hong Kong, my best friend by my side. You couldn't tell us a single, solitary thing; the hotel was lovely—on par with the Mandarin Oriental in New York, which meant it was first class all the way, with beautifully appointed rooms I'd never before seen or experienced. The shades and curtains opened electronically with the push of a button; this twenty-year-old girl, a product of southeast DC, had never seen anything like that. "This right here is it—exactly how we're supposed to be treated," I said to Tracie, who nodded furiously in agreement. "I can get used to this!"

• • •

It was my strong work ethic that earned me a spot on the *Dreamgirls* stage, but it was my confidence and hustle that got me into the camera line of a scene in Spike Lee's *Malcolm X,* smack-dab in front of Denzel Washington. That particular hustle started back at Howard, during a workshop Spike gave at our university's drama department. Spike was the gawd back then—an African American filmmaker whose unflinching, unapologetic commentary on black American life not only ushered in a cinematic and cultural renaissance for moviegoers, but also opened doors for black folk both in front of and behind the camera. By the time he made it to Howard, he'd already gotten crazy accolades for *She's Gotta Have It, School Daze, Do the Right Thing,* and *Mo' Better Blues,* and everybody on campus was trying to get next to him, knowing he was still casting for *Malcolm X.* So my girlfriend Tracie and I got ourselves all super-cute and hightailed it over to the lecture hall. Though we tried, we couldn't get anywhere near Spike. We settled for making nice with a guy in his entourage, some bugaboo who was trying to holler. I practically held my nose and gagged while I shoved both my and Tracie's headshots into his hands. "Look, just take these pictures and give them to Spike," I said, with an attitude and half a smile.

I knew he wasn't a casting agent, and I have no idea if he actually gave those pictures to Spike Lee or not, but in my mind, what we did worked. A few weeks later, I was in dance class doing pliés when Tracie put in a frantic call to the drama department office and made herself sound super-official. She told whoever answered the phone that Spike Lee wanted me in a movie. The girl from the office hoofed it down the stairs and burst into the studio with the news. "Taraji!" she said, barely able to catch her breath. "You got a call from New York about *Malcolm X!*"

"Oh my God," I screamed, cupping my hands over my mouth and falling down to my knees like I'd just hit the lottery and won an Oscar, an Emmy, and a Grammy all in the same night. The class erupted into a gaggle of squeals and high fives as I hurriedly squeezed myself into my street clothes: a fabulous all-leopard outfit featuring a vintage coat with a matching skirt and, yes, the hat. I tipped out of that dance class fresh dressed like a million bucks, hopped in my car, and crushed a few speeding laws rushing to my apartment to pack my clothes and hightail it to New York on a seventy-five-dollar plane ticket my mother purchased for me because as I had to pay both my rent and tuition, I was too broke to buy it on my own.

When I think about that particular moment, I fall out in fits of laughter because, really, the audacity of me—some drama undergrad with no professional experience outside of the Howard University stage, a ThighMaster infomercial, and my job singing Tina Turner songs on that dinner barge—thinking I could book a job off a résumé and headshot! Spike Lee had never, to my knowledge, been to one of my plays, he'd never pulled up a seat on the *Spirit of Washington* while I belted out "Proud Mary," and he sure as hell didn't know me from a hole in the wall. I was wet behind the ears—didn't know any better. I just knew somehow I'd impressed Spike and he wanted me. My mother, too, was in lockstep on that assessment: just before she drove me to the airport, she was racing around her office, telling anyone within the sound of her voice, "Spike Lee picked my baby to star in his movie!" In our minds, Taraji P. Henson was about to blow up.

I arrived in New York with my outdated suitcase, big and burgundy and all kinds of wrong, dressed in that same head-to-toe leopard suit I was wearing when I got the call from Tracie back at dance class, looking country as shit, standing on the sidewalk outside Lincoln Center, sucking in that thick air and crackling energy buzzing like lightning all around me while I waited for

Tracie to pick me up. I wanted to shout to everyone who walked by, "I'm starring in Spike Lee's new movie!" But I knew enough to at least play it a little bit cool on those streets, where New Yorkers are always in a rush and woefully unimpressed by pretty much everything in general and wet-nosed tourists in particular; I saved my ninja kicks and cheerleader jumps for Tracie, who also had secured a role.

. . .

Tracie and I tracked down our contact, some lady with a clipboard and an attitude lording over the "extras" base camp blocks away from the Harlem set where the scene was to be filmed. In my mind, I'd envisioned that she would usher us to a quiet room somewhere on the set, where Spike would welcome us, offer us something to eat, then sit us down to go over the script and ask us what, exactly, was the motivation we'd have to employ to get into character. Instead, the lady with the clipboard pointed, and at the end of her finger was a dusty tent crowded with random people sitting around, mindlessly chewing on snacks and jockeying for empty chairs.

We were extras. *Extras*. Chile, I believed I'd had a starring role. I was so ahead of myself.

To understand the gravity of this situation, you need to understand the life of an extra. For the most part, it sucks. Rain, hail, sleet, or snow, you're rounded up like cattle and herded into a small area where you and a bunch of strangers sit practically on top of one another while you wait for hours to get your hair and makeup done, then a few hours more to get your costume just right, and then a few more hours on top of that waiting for strategic placement somewhere on the set, where your every movement is choreographed down to the angle in which you should point your pinky toe—all in exchange for some snacks and a couple of dollars for your pocket. The perks? Few. Except that if your people squint their eyes a little bit, lean in real close to the screen, and get really handy with the pause button, somebody might see you, which'll make you hood famous, but not much else besides one step closer to your Screen Actors Guild (SAG) card if you're lucky enough to get a SAG-sanctioned gig.

I needed more than that, though. I wasn't trying to be a blip on anybody's screen; we needed to hatch a plan. Tracie and I hustled ourselves over to the snack table for the non-SAG-card extras, then found our way over to two empty seats and understood rather quickly what was our lot. I bit into my cookie and surveyed the landscape. The SAG-card extras were throwing shade, acting like they had one up on those of us who were nonunion. "See, this shit right here, I can't do," I huffed. "The only thing they got different," I said, nodding toward the SAG extras, "is a bagel. We gotta eat the cookies and drink the Tang, and they got bagels and orange juice, which ain't that much better, so go sit down somewhere."

Anyone who's ever been an extra on a television or film production knows I'm telling the God's honest truth. That's the grind. No one in charge is purposefully mean, and extras know not to take any of it personally. They know they're on set to do what it is they've been asked to do, and they get the job done. And those in charge know that without them, our movies and television shows wouldn't look real. In other words, we need extras.

. . .

Knowing that struggle firsthand, I make a point of treating extras on my sets with the respect and dignity they deserve. I make
them laugh, make them feel welcomed, and, in some cases, like
a former waitress who tips well because she knows the struggle,
I fight for equitable treatment among the extras because, hell, it's
only right. Take, for instance, what happened on the set of *Seasons
of Love*, the 2014 Lifetime original movie I executive produced
and starred in with LeToya Luckett. One day while strolling the
set, I overheard someone, presumably a SAG-card-carrying extra,
order a non-SAG-card extra off a food line. "Only SAG extras
can eat here," he sneered. With flashbacks to the hierarchy on
the *Malcolm X* set, I did what I could to make it so that everybody
under the extras tent felt wanted: I ordered a waffle truck and invited the extras to dig in. "Everybody, eat up," I said. "This is for
whoever wants waffles, no matter if you're SAG or not."

On the New Orleans set of *From the Rough,* the movie in
which I starred as Dr. Catana Starks, the first woman to coach a
men's college golf team, I actually got a little miffed about how
no one seemed to care that the extras were literally baking in the
hot summer sun, with nary a tent, umbrella, or drop of water in
sight to help keep them comfortable while they waited hours to
play their parts. "If y'all don't get a tent on those people right now
and get them some water and some chairs, I'm calling SAG!" I
barked. No one was trying to make them uncomfortable on purpose; someone pointed out to me that the production assistants
were working on providing that critical relief to the extras, but

they were just dragging on and on. "Get it out there, shit," I said, stalking off.

. . .

As an extra, though, you have to learn how to take care of yourself, too. And that's what Tracie and I did on the set of *Malcolm X*. Within minutes of sitting under that tent, Tracie and I were plotting how to go from being extras eating donuts in Spike's and Denzel's eyes to actresses who would be so impressive, so magnetic, Spike would be all, "It's you two!" and Denzel would chime in, "Damn, it's y'all!" We were trying to work this thing. That's when the hustle "Operation Get Seen in Denzel's Scene" went into full effect.

We were hired to be in the crowd listening to Malcolm X deliver a sermon about cops being the "new KKK" on a Harlem street corner, and we made it our mission to get to the front row, right in front of Denzel and especially right in front of the camera. It was going to take some work because there were a lot of extras. But Tracie and I had some ideas. First and foremost, we needed to look the part, which meant we had to make especially nice with two of the most important departments on the set: wardrobe, and hair and makeup.

"Oh, you're going to have to cover up that hair," the stylist in the hair department said as she circled around my chair, checking out my then-blond tresses.

I reached down into my bag and pulled out a black wig. A trained actress, I had done my research. I knew that blond wasn't fashionable in Harlem in the sixties, and if I wanted to get noticed, I'd have to look the part. "That's right, baby," the hair stylist said as she fit the wig over my head, instantly transforming me into a conservative sixties housewife. "Come ready to work!"

As for costumes, we got lucky. Yvette, a friend and fellow Howard alum who had been in a few productions with me back at school, was working in the costume department. She took extra care to make sure we had the flyest clothes—some vintage pieces that really put us in the moment of Malcolm's movement. "Put these gloves on," she said before sending us off. "Nobody had long acrylic hook nails back then. They see that and you're going to the back."

The true hustle came when it was time to jockey for a position up front. Getting there wasn't such a hard thing to do: we just ducked and dived and excused our way toward the front, then were escorted the rest of the way because of how we were dressed. Staying up front, though, was an entirely different thing. There we were, giggling and wiggling and ready for somebody to yell "action!" when all of a sudden one of the buildings working as a backdrop to Malcolm's speech started smoking. "All the extras back up!" a man yelled into a bullhorn, as a line of set assistants spread their arms and motioned us back. Tracie and I weren't having it, though; we locked arms and refused to move. "Do you know what it took for us to get up here?" I asked out loud. "This is our spot. We're not going anywhere."

We stood firm, even as fire trucks roared onto the scene, even as the firemen told us to step away from the sidewalk, even as that smoke billowed up into the air. "They gonna put that fire out and I'm going to be right here," I insisted, grabbing Tracie's arm a little tighter. I didn't care if it was a five alarm; I wasn't going to leave my spot. "My mama took time out of her schedule and dropped me off, she ain't got no money and she paid seventy five dollars for this ticket," I yelled. "She gonna see me in this movie!"

By the time they gave the powers that be the all clear—nothing happened to the building; there was smoke but no actual fire—Tracie and I were standing right there in front of Denzel, on the front row. Evidence of my hustle? Watch *Malcolm X* closely; in that scene, when the camera pans out to the audience, guess who you'll see? Me and Tracie, front row and center. The camera stops on us for a hot minute, and later, while Malcolm is talking, you can hear us, too. Listen closely for "Yassir, preach, Malcolm!" That's me and my big mouth. For the longest time, my mother would perch herself on her bed, right in front of her television, with the remote between her fingers, pausing the scene so she could see her baby's face staring back at her.

That's what hustle gets you. Giving up isn't ever an option for me; whatever the obstacle, best believe I'll run headfirst through it, climb over it, or crawl under it to get exactly what I want.

• • •

Despite all the newfound success, there was one professor who was thoroughly unimpressed with my onstage antics: one Professor Vera Katz, an older woman with a shock of red hair and a rasp in her throat. Even today, she emails me notes on all the projects I work on, and sometimes she even calls. Leaning on all the bravado she possesses to get me to understand where she's coming from, she'll say, "Taraji, I see you thinking. I love it. I love it! You're always thinking. Your eyes tell the truth. I see your moments before the lines. I see where you're coming from. It's beautiful."

This is music to my ears now, but her accolades were a long time coming. I gave Professor Katz hell when I was at Howard, and she gave it right back to me in spades. Every time she opened her mouth to tell me how to be onstage, I would grimace and give her Black Girl attitude that screamed, "You don't know me! You don't know my struggle! Power to the people!" I'd be so disrespectful to her—show up late to her class, talk all through it when I bothered to be on time—she would kick my ass right on out. "Miss Henson, you look really cute in your thigh-high red boots and your matching jacket, but you're late. Get out!" she would say, pointing at the door.

Still, I wanted her approval, because she was the main one at Howard who refused to give it to me. It doesn't matter if practically an entire audience of hundreds of people stand on their chairs and jump and holler and scream your name as they cheer you wildly on, you will notice only the one person sitting in the chair with her lips pursed and her hands clasped on her lap, giving you a dead-eyed stare that screams, "They may be impressed, but I'm not." That was Professor Katz. She was thoroughly uninspired by my hustle and made a point of letting me know that when it came to the craft, I was more con artist than actress. "Go deeper!" she would yell, interrupting my class monologues to chastise me for leaning on tricks to grab the attention of my peers. Always my instinct would be to talk loud, throw my body into it—to make the scene, the lines, grand. But Professor Katz would have none of it; she saw a deeper actress. A thinking actress. She insisted that I consider what happened to my character in the moments *before* the scene, so that when I opened my mouth, I was responding not to what I'd memorized from the page, but to the emotions the experience conjured. "No, no, no, I don't believe it!" she would yell, interrupting my lines. "You're clever and you make good choices, but what's behind those choices? What does your character want? You have to think like humans think. Don't stop thinking just because somebody wrote the words on a page. You're not a robot. You still have to think!"

Understand, getting ripped apart and torn to shreds was frightening in front of a classroom of peers who audition and fight for the same roles as you. But Professor Katz didn't care about such things. To hell with my ego. She seemed to take great pleasure in drawing blood.

Our conflict came to a head over my portrayal in a play penned by a fellow Howard alum, Guinea Bennett, a good friend of mine who, after graduation, went on to found the Soul Rep Theater Company in Dallas, Texas. Guinea and I were members of a collective of crazy, artsy seventies babies who dressed alike, listened to the same music, and, in the way that kindred spirits do, created together. We even had our own monikers, cherry-picked from names popular in our birth decade: Leroy, Tyrone, Juanita, Suge. I was Cookie Gwendolyn Jones. Yes, "Cookie." We called our little collective Soul Nation, and Guinea wrote and produced a play for us, *Cracking Up,* about a group of girls in college dealing with heavy issues such as pregnancy, drug dealing, and several other societal ills surrounding our campus—a play so beautifully penned that the Howard drama department agreed to let us produce it on its stage. That play was a hit; we sold out every night, with students from the fine arts department and beyond lining up to come see us. My character was a standout: I had blond braids and was loud and brash and in-your-face, and I got all the laughs of the night with my one-liners. I was the star. And every night when I stood up on that stage and took a bow, I would say a silent, *Yeah, take that, Vera Katz. You're always giving me all that flack in your class, but look what I did. I'm all they talk about . . .*

Ego much?

The next time I had her class, I strutted in as if I owned the place. I couldn't wait to rub my success in her face. But in typical fashion, Professor Katz quietly broke me down. "Miss Henson, you were loud and over the top. It was too big." Even with all the accolades and applause, even when everybody else was laughing and falling for my jokes, Professor Katz was making it clear my tricks didn't work for her. I was missing what was on the page. I was a fraud.

The rest of my time there, I worked to get her approval. The last monologue I did for her was a quiet one. There was no yelling, no grand physical gestures; only pure emotion and restrained intensity, which was so much more difficult to do than any of the other tricks I'd employed up until that moment. I'd finally internalized everything she'd been saying to me over our year together. When I said my last word and the class's applause died down, Professor Katz stood and gave me an easy smile. "All that time, I thought you were fighting and not listening," she said quietly.

"I was," I said. "I just had an odd way of showing it."

We reconciled, and years later, at an awards ceremony where she was being honored and I was a host, I apologized to her. "I know I gave you hell," I said. "But you are a huge reason why I'm so successful in the business. You challenged me to be a thinker, to always stay alive and be in the moment. To respect the craft."

. . .

I meant that, too. I'd like to think that the choices I've made were informed by the way Professor Katz and my other acting coaches, Jemal McNeil and Tony Greco, who taught legendary methods like the Meisner Technique, trained me to engage the work; through them, I learned that hustling as an actress isn't just about flicking your hair, batting your eyelashes, wearing the cutest outfit, and plowing through the words; it's about understanding and working the spaces and angles between what is obvious to everyone else, and using those quiet moments to stand out. To win.

That is the hallmark of a true hustler.

5
My One and Only Love Story

We had that Jody and Yvette *Baby Boy* kind of love—passionate, raw, and "young, dumb, and out of control," like the tragically immature, stunted main character in John Singleton's critically acclaimed, urban cult classic. That's what you get, though, when you mix youth with inexperience, shake in some hood, and boil it with a heap of hot tempers: an intoxicating brew of tragic ghetto love.

The truth is we didn't stand a chance.

But I didn't know any of that when I first laid eyes on Mark in the summer of 1987. I saw him in the lobby of the Riverside Theater in Riverside, Maryland, standing there with a bunch of his friends, eating popcorn and staring at me with these great big ol' eyes as if he were in a trance. Without saying a single word, he made me feel as if I were the most beautiful girl in the world. I was seventeen and had only had one boyfriend up until then, a guy I'd dated two years earlier. He was sweet enough, but he wasn't all that enthusiastic about the limitations that came with dating Bernice Gordon's baby girl, particularly the "No Boys in the House When Mama's Not Home" rule and especially the "She's a Virgin and Will Stay That Way" decree. Let's just say I wasn't all that surprised when my first boyfriend, who was already sexually active when we began dating, announced he was calling it quits because he didn't want to cheat on me. I was fine with his decision. I wasn't ready for all the stakes that came with teenage pregnancy, or single parenting, for that matter. On those subjects and many others, my mother had instilled the fear of God in me. The very thought of going against her wishes petrified me, what with all the threats to knock my teeth out of my head and to slap me into next Tuesday. My auntie would hear her talking crazy to me and she'd get genuinely concerned: "Why are you talking to her like that? You need to stop that, Bernice!" But I knew she had cause for all that tough talk: I was a young girl in a wild city, and she needed to keep me in check so the streets wouldn't try me. She never had to make good on the threats; all she had to do was shoot me that look and I knew—I just knew—whatever it was I was doing, I better pull it together and stop it. When she cut her eyes, I knew she meant business. I wasn't that kid who was wont to cause trouble or go against her mother's wishes. If she said I wasn't ready for sex and shouldn't do it, she didn't have to tell me but once.

Deep down, I knew I wasn't ready then, either. By the time I met Mark, though, this caterpillar had blossomed into a butterfly who knew from the second our energy mingled in that lobby that here was someone for whom it was worth breaking a few rules. I could tell this just by looking into his eyes that night at the movie theater. It wasn't my modus operandi to roll up on strange guys and start talking to them. But Mark? He was cinnamon brown with a mouthful of the whitest, most perfectly straight teeth that spread into the widest, most beautiful smile, the perfect complement to all that swag dripping off of him. He was stylish and different, with a hint of danger to him. I liked it. Plus, he very smoothly laid out the red carpet just for me. I figured I might as well strut on it. As we locked each other into our respective lines of vision, I walked right up to him and snatched his popcorn out of his hands.

"Is this for me?" I asked coyly.

"You can have some if you want it," he said easily, shifting his body against the wall, looking right into my eyes.

Minutes later, he and his boys, who were there to see a different film from what my girls and I had come to see, were following us into our movie theater. I can't even remember what we saw that night; I was much too focused on Mark, who was sitting directly behind me, flirting, whispering in my ear, playing with my hair, and giving me cute love taps on my back and shoulders like we were first-graders. He barely had to form the words in his mouth to ask me for my number; my digits were already written on a wrinkled piece of notebook paper, ready to slide his way.

He called me the next day, and we talked about everything under the sun and nothing at all, long after I'd crawled up under my covers, long, even, after my mother burst into my room yelling, "I know you're not still on the phone!" A few days after that, right after we'd finished killing the all-you-can-eat buffet at

Denny's, he kissed me, smiled, then took off into the aisle of the parking lot and did a series of cartwheels on the asphalt. When he somersaulted for me, I fell for him. Hard.

It didn't take long for us to become exclusive. We never really said we were, either; we just fell into it. He was my first love— the first man I gave myself to emotionally, mentally, physically. I knew he considered me his woman because he was taking me around his friends all the time and we spent quite a bit of time at his house, where his mother always welcomed me with open arms. She liked that I was polite and respectful—that the moment I stepped through that front door, I'd make a beeline to wherever she was, give her a hug, and talk to her politely and with respect. To this day, she'll say that's what she always loved about me—that I never acted like any of those hot-tailed girls who'd go over there and ignore her, like her son was the one paying the rent and light bill. That's not the way I was raised. If there's grown folk in the room, I speak.

I wanted a forever love with Mark. If that man had said he was ready to have babies and get married, I would have had a pastor and an obstetrician lined up within the hour. Without hesitation, I would have marched right down the aisle with him. I wanted to be married because that's the one thing I was sure of: that I would make a good wife and a hell of a mother. I wanted Mark to be my husband.

Mark saw things differently.

There was some sense to it: though he was a year older than me, he wasn't ready for "I dos" and babies. Hell, we were babies ourselves. While I was determined to move forward, Mark was still trying to find his footing in the world. College wasn't an option; Mark tried it for a semester or two, but he hated school and wasn't up for juggling classes and work. Of course, without a formal college education, his employment options were limited, and even when he did get hold of a decent job working in the receiving and packaging department at Washington National Airport, he barely made enough to pay rent on his own apartment, keep food in his refrigerator, pay his bills, and have a little left over to enjoy his life. He was trapped. Damn if he was going to get a wife and baby caught up in that web while he was still trying to figure it all out.

In 1987, when I went off to my freshman year at North Carolina A&T, our relationship, in my mind, was solid. Though we would be separated, we were ready to conquer the world together. But by the time I finished up my spring semester, he was already pulling away from me. Chalk it up to inexperience or being drunk in love, but I was too blind to see that we were growing apart and that his heart wasn't in it like it was in the beginning. In just one short academic year, we were through. He tried to let me down gently, but I was intent on fighting for our love. "You're better than me," he said one night while I lay in his arms. "You need to leave me alone."

His words felt like a punch to my gut. I'd seen enough men in our neighborhood give up, especially after they felt like the world had turned its back on them. Hell, I'd seen it happen with my own family, with my own father, whose temper, fired up from returning home from Vietnam to a country that refused to treat him as an equal, had landed him in jail on one too many occasions. He would get mad, get into an argument with someone, and the next thing we knew, he would be locked up. That was an entrée to his dance with poverty; a black man with a record can't count on a good job and a paycheck—not when he has to check a box on a job application that identifies him as a former convict. Where there is no job, there is no money, and where there is no money, there is trouble. My father was a good guy, but his demons haunted him, and he struggled to escape their wrath on his own.

In my mind, all Mark needed was a hand up. I wasn't about to leave him in the elements. That was my man. I was going to fight for him.

"Look, I know it's hard out here, but we can do it together," I insisted as I hugged him a little tighter. "I'm working," I said, referring to the job I had waitressing on the boat. "I'm going to be making some decent money soon and we'll be able to get us a place, and when I finish school, there'll be even more for us. Let me help you." At the time I was pursuing that engineering degree, and while I wasn't on course to give Steve Jobs a run for his money, I always knew how to work, how to hustle.

I kissed his lips and neck and tickled him a little, looking to lighten the mood, but his energy was off. It was clear there would be no cartwheels to express his love like he'd done that time in the parking lot when we first met. Something had shifted. And then he got dark.

I didn't mean to, but while I was trying to lighten the mood, I reached up to play with a gold chain he was wearing and accidentally broke it, and Mark got angry—the maddest I'd ever seen him. He raised his voice and said the meanest things. I couldn't understand where the sudden rage was coming from.

"But I love you," I insisted, crying. "I thought you loved me, too!"

He didn't. That fight—simple yet decisive—was the end of us.

Who was I fooling? By the next weekend, I'd climbed into my cutest, shortest dress and my highest heels and made sure my hair and makeup were just right and grabbed my girlfriend Tracie and went down there to Chapter III, the hottest dance club in DC, tucked in the shadow of the Capitol. "I just need to get out this house," I told her.

"Uh-huh," Tracie said, laughing. "You know we're going over there because Mark is going to be there."

"Whatever," I huffed. "You know the drill."

She was right, I knew Mark would be there, and I wanted him to see me—to know what he'd given away. And I'm not going to front: I wanted to see him, too, to win him back. Today, I know that in marching myself to this lair, I was giving away all my power. But at nineteen, this seemed like a brilliant idea.

It wasn't.

Mark got all in his feelings when he spotted me dancing and grinning in front of some guy who was smiling back at me and making it clear that he was interested. Mark marched right up to us, snatched my arm, and grabbed me up like he was my daddy and I was his errant five-year-old child.

"Don't get cute," he said, sneering.

"What are you talking about?" I yelled, pulling away. "You're the one who wanted to break up."

"That doesn't mean you come to the club looking like that, throwing yourself at other random dudes!" he screamed directly in my face.

By now we were causing quite the scene. The crowd started leaning in to see what all the commotion was about, and there was some jostling and more yelling, and Tracie was trying to get between us to calm me down and Mark was waving his arms and roaring. It quickly escalated out of control. No punches were thrown, but there was enough of a commotion to draw the attention of the club's bouncers, who made quick work of moving bodies to get to the center of the action.

Next thing I know, the bouncers put us out of the club, but Mark gets to stay! The bouncers didn't touch him. But the girls? Side-eye. They had us hemmed in and pinned up and we were screaming and cursing and trying to pull back our arms and tug down our miniskirts, which had risen so high in all that ruckus that our asses were showing! I tried desperately to pry the bouncer's vise grip off my wrist to stop him from making my new watch dig into my skin; that was a piece I'd just got from Cosmo, a trendy store where Tracie and I got our fly gear. We knew we were cute when we climbed into our outfits from Cosmo, destined for big things. But on that night, we were just some hood rats starting fights and getting booted out the club. Everybody was staring as that bouncer dragged us through the crowd. "Shut up, with your weave," one man yelled, practically spitting at us, as we passed by. Tracie managed to yank herself away from the bouncer long enough to grab her hair and shove it toward that man's face.

"Yo, this is my hair, bitch!" she screamed, before the bouncer grabbed her again and recommenced to pushing and dragging us to the front of the club. He pressed his man hands on our backs and shoved us out the door.

"Get out!" he said. "And don't come back." I was undone. I had always been the good girl. I followed the rules. Any drama I

encountered was usually on the stage. This was new for me. And
I wanted no part of it.

But guess who was back at the club, in line with shades on, the
very next weekend?

. . .

There were plenty of examples of marriages that lasted in my
immediate family, but no one was telling us to pull up a chair
and get some firsthand instruction on how to make relationships
work. And closer to home, in the rough-and-tumble neighborhood where Mark and I lived, single mothers struggled and made
do, even and especially since the presence of fathers and father
figures was in all too short supply. People went together, sure.
That was human. But staying together? That was a whole different beast. Youth, inexperience, environment, and a lack of relationship role models made my union with Mark a recipe for
disaster.

Still, I wanted him. And I tried my best to get that through his
thick skull, even after he grabbed me and so enraged me that I got
kicked out of the club. "I don't understand why you want to break
up. We're going places," I reasoned. "I love you. We can do this
together. I won't let you fall."

By now Mark was seeing things differently and wasted not
one second entertaining my "you and me against the world" fantasy. "Let me explain it to you like this," he said. "You're like an
old favorite bag. When I don't want to use it anymore, I put it
away on a shelf."

Now, I know a dis when I hear one, and I've never been one

to hold back my tongue, but when I heard that I was rendered speechless. I admit, I didn't know what, exactly, to make of what he was saying: Was it that he loved me, but he wasn't ready to be with me? Was it that I was old faithful, the one he would always remember as "The One"? Was I the old bag that you used to love but now that it's all old and raggedy, you keep it around for sentimental reasons, but as soon as you get your check, you head to the store in search of something new?

"Forget him," my friend Pam said, seething, after I recounted Mark's analogy. "You're not an old-ass bag!" She was pissed. I was simply heartbroken.

· · ·

It would be a good year before we got back together, and for a while in those months, our lives changed in immeasurable ways, with my trajectory rising as Mark's remained stagnant. By then, in the summer of 1991, I'd moved out from my father's basement and into my own apartment, I'd gotten myself another good job singing and performing on a cruise boat, and I'd finally gotten up the cash I needed to pay off my tuition at and get my transcript from North Carolina A&T and pay my way at Howard University, where I'd transferred in as a theater major. I had my act together.

Mark, however, was still struggling. In the time that he was busy breaking up with me, he'd managed to get not one, but two women pregnant, just months apart. His daughters came into this world with a father who was increasingly overwhelmed by all of his responsibilities.

Though I knew about all of this—the other women, the babies, the struggling, his increased despondence—I still wanted him back, and eventually he felt the same. It's not just that he was charming, that he was beautiful, that he had swag and knew how to dress, or that he smelled good. It wasn't that he'd made it clear that the old bag he'd tucked up on the shelf in the back of his closet was in fashion again. It was that I saw the good in him. So I forgave him, even though he wasn't trying to call a thing a thing. I was too busy giving our relationship—indeed, us—my all to get hung up on the breakups or the titles. I even accepted and embraced his babies, hanging out with and helping care for them when they visited Mark. How could I be anything different under those circumstances? I was maternal in that way; I love babies. But even more, it wasn't an option for me to reject my man's children. How, after all, can you love a man and not his offspring? Plus, I'm a firm believer that when you agree to take somebody back, you open your arms not just to the relationship, but everything your significant other is bringing back with them. If I was going to love him fully, I was going to have to love his children.

Still, no matter the intentions, no matter the effort, we just couldn't get our shit together. We were reckless and dramatic. Thank God we didn't have social media and camera phones back then. We'd have definitely been all over Facebook, Twitter, and Instagram had someone caught that one Valentine's Day when I was ringing Mark's phone all afternoon and he didn't answer. "Where the hell are you?" I sneered into the answering machine. "You can call me when you need the car and all that, but you can't call me on Valentine's Day?"

All I saw was bloodred as I sped over to his place in my Pulsar, and that bloodred in my eyes began to pulse when I looked up at his window and saw lights flickering. The television was on. I saw action—life going on up there. Then I saw his friend Jerry look out the window. Damn if I was going to stand down on that street and let him get away with ignoring my phone calls.

He lived in a building that required you get buzzed in, but I knew how to snatch the security entrance door just right and get through all of that. In a flash, I was up the stairs, banging on the door, demanding he let me in. "Open this door!" I yelled as I rained my pounding fist on his apartment door. "I saw Jerry looking out the window and I can hear the TV. Open up!"

Finally, Mark snatched open his door. Standing just behind him was one of the mothers of his children, coat on, their baby in a car seat, preparing to leave. The sight of them made my heart stop; I was crushed. There he was standing in his apartment with his little family, and there I was, standing on the outside of his home and his heart on Valentine's Day. I was broken.

"Y'all having family day, bitch, and it's Valentine's? For real?" I yelled.

Now, being mature and rational with the hindsight of a grown-up, I can look back at that moment and acknowledge that maybe, just maybe, she was there for something other than a Valentine's Day celebration. She could have been picking up some money for the baby, or maybe she'd dropped her child off for a visit with her father and was there, at that moment, to pick up her kid. Either of those scenarios would have made perfect sense. But there is no rational thinking when you're immature, in love, and desperate to mend what's irreparable. Rather than talk it out, we commenced to tussling. With all the commotion, neighbors were peeking out of doors and telling us to shut up and threatening to call the police. He was trying to get me to leave, but I was too busy pulling curses up from deep inside my chest—words I was using to cut him down to the white meat. We wrestled all the way to the elevator. Finally, a neighbor yelled down the hallway. "Look, they called the cops. Y'all better get out of here!"

I hopped in my car so fast, head spinning, clothes disheveled, head pounding. I'd had enough; right then, I decided it was over. I went home, played some Phyllis Hyman on my stereo, and drank my wine to get over his ass once and for all. Two hours later, he was back at my door, begging me to let him back in.

. . .

This is my one love story—all at once extraordinary and ordinary. It is the song that women sing every day, the lyrics melancholy but hopeful, sometimes angry, reflective. Always full of longing. I wanted Mark. He wanted me back. But the divide between us was too far to cross, and neither of us had the tools—communication skills, trust, focus, patience—to build that bridge to get one another. The truth is we were very much like the main characters in *Baby Boy,* the movie in which Jody, portrayed by Tyrese Gibson, and Yvette, my character, consistently struggled to overcome issues with infidelity, commitment, single parenting, and immaturity. But unlike in the movie, in which Jody gets himself together, gives up his immature ways, and commits to being with Yvette and their son, ours was not a happy Hollywood ending. The truth is, Mark wasn't through breaking my heart, and to this day, I am still recovering. The hard truth is, I allowed it all.

6

Single Mother

O ur breakup was short-lived. I knew I was pregnant that night in the summer of 1993 when my baby was conceived. After we made love, I fell asleep in Mark's arms and had a dream so vivid, it should have been pinstriped and in Technicolor: I was sitting on the bed in my apartment, back straight as an arrow, a smile as bright as the sunlight streaming through the window, with my hands outstretched. In them was a tight, tiny bundle wrapped in blue. "I'm pregnant," I blurted out when I opened my eyes. Mark, freshly showered and shaved, was sitting at the foot of the bed, pulling on socks, getting himself ready for work. He didn't even bother looking up at me. "Yeah, whatever, Taraji. No you ain't."

Sure enough, God had planted a little butterfly in my cocoon. Lord, I was so happy. Not in the sense of some pop-cultural fascination with baby bumps, cute pregnancy clothes, and balloon-filled baby showers, or a naive teenager's obsession with wanting a tiny, powder-scented, doll-like little one to hug on and snuggle; I wasn't sitting in class, drawing pink bubble hearts around a long list of baby names in my English notebook and imagining what my pregnant belly would look like or which cute boy in my school would make the prettiest little girl. I was more into the *Leave It to Beaver* aspect that came with parenthood—the care-taking part of it all. This was the family dynamic I saw around me: when I looked at my extended family, I saw mothers keeping beautiful homes and raising their children with stern, loving hands, and fathers protecting and providing for their families. Sure, my mother raised me all on her own, but she was no different from the majority of the women in my family who were married with kids. All of them relished their role as their family's caregiver and nurturer, having a hot breakfast ready for their kids in the mornings, sending their children to school freshly dressed like a million bucks, making sure that when company came through, not so much as a speck of dust was on the coffee table, doing what it took to remind their men that they were kings of their castles. That vision of domesticity was ingrained in my DNA, and I've never strayed far from the ideal. Even as a little girl, I would set up all my ultragirly toys—my play iron and ironing board, my kid kitchen, my pretend vacuum cleaner, all of that—and imagine I was the lady of the house, cooking dinner and doing laundry while waiting for my husband to get in from work. Barbie? Please—she couldn't do a thing for me but remind me that I didn't have much. Barbie had it all, condos, shoes, cars. Hell, just having Barbie would have broken the bank, considering all the accessories you had to buy to make her extra fly. I was much more into changing pampers on doll babies, pretend feeding them bottles and smushed applesauce and peas, and then play rocking them to sleep. That instinct—that desire for motherhood, marriage, and domesticity—only grew stronger after puberty hit and stronger still after I trotted off to Howard in pursuit of an acting career. It bloomed right along with every other facet of me.

When I found out I was pregnant, I was still a junior at Howard but in a good place—paying my way through school, living in my own apartment, making good money as a supervisor on the *Odyssey*, another dinner cruise ship that operated on the waters of the Potomac. I'd even started making some noise in theater at Howard, getting my due onstage and pulling in some cash at gigs around town. What's more, the moment we confirmed with a doctor that I was, indeed, pregnant, the Mark I fell in love with showed up and put in the work to support our unborn child and me. Truly he was an angel: he made sure I ate, picked me up from and took me to my doctor's appointments and class and grocery shopping, rubbed my back when it was sore, and fell down to his knees right beside me when I prayed for our baby. He was always quick with bringing the fun to it all; pillow fights were standard, playful name-calling essential. He kept me laughing. Content. He even started showing up to family functions with me, something he'd never done in all the years we'd been together. My aunties would hug and kiss him, and my uncles would slap him on the back and make him feel welcome. I'd be by his side, beaming, grateful that he was there and totally saying to myself, *Finally we're going to be a real family. He gets it.* We saw nothing but good things for our baby. And for us.

Of course, my mother saw my pregnancy a little differently. When I told her the news, she freaked out. It was, "Oh my God,

this is the end of your career!" and "Oh my God, your life is over!"
She threw in "Oh my God, how will you manage all this?" too,
convinced that because Mark and I were not married, I would be
every bit as emotionally and financially drained as she was as a
single mom. The wedding ring—and the commitment that came
with it—mattered. Her concerns were valid, I guess. She knew
firsthand, after all, how hard it was to be a single parent, to juggle
motherhood and a career without the stability that comes with
a second parent consistently present, and to be physically, emotionally, and financially accountable to raising a child alone. She
knew, too, the pressure that both a mother and her child feels
when they're the ones that everybody is whispering about—when
they're the ones carrying the burdens of stereotypes and low expectations and the avalanche of statistics that insist that kids from
"broken" homes won't make it.

I knew the stakes, too. I am, after all, the product of a single-
parent household—the only child in my extended family to grow
up in a nontraditional home in the inner city. My mother constantly struggled under the mental, emotional, and financial weight
of providing for herself and me, and I felt that pressure every time
my mother had to go to work rather than stay home with me,
every time we left my aunts' spacious homes in the suburbs and
came back to our tiny apartment in the inner city, every time my
mother had to tell me, with tears in her eyes, that she just couldn't
afford things that seemed to be a given in two-parent households,
from exotic vacations to fancy clothes to college tuition. I borrow
from Langston Hughes's poem "Mother to Son" in saying this:
Life ain't been no crystal stair for my mother or for me.

Still, there was never a question about whether I could or

would keep my baby. When those two red lines slowly crept into view on that home pregnancy test, there wasn't a second of hesitation. I knew God intended it and that I could handle what was to come. I didn't want anybody crying for me, even and especially my overly worried mother. Besides, Mark and I were still together, and though we were not married, I fully believed he would be a good father to our baby and a sound partner in parenting. When my mother freaked out, I put the grown woman in my voice and let her know what was up: "Why you over there crying and stuff?" I asked, annoyed. "I can't have negativity. I won't have it! This baby is not a disease. You're up here acting like I'm fifteen and in high school. I'm twenty-four years old, in college, paying my own way, and I'm on the dean's list. There are other things you could be freaking out about; this ain't it.

"I don't need anything from you except your unconditional support," I added. "I'm having a happy, healthy baby and I'm thrilled about it, and if you and your family aren't down for that, I'm not coming around."

I thought she was going to come out of the phone and choke me; you don't talk to black mamas like that. Instead, she dried up those tears real quick.

She was the undercard fight, though. Breaking the news to my father? That was the main event. Of him, I was scared. He had gotten his act together. He was a born-again Christian by then, firm in his beliefs about what was moral, and I was about to tell him that his little girl was with child, thus confirming unequivocally that I was having premarital sex. Surely, I would incur a wrath of biblical proportions. Even my stepmother was scared for me.

"Did you tell Henson yet?" she asked when I called and broke the news.

"No," I said meekly. "I'm telling you first."

She paused. "Okay," she said all slow. "Hold on, here you go."

She handed the phone to my father and before he could get the receiver to his ear, he was asking, "What's up? What's up?" loud and obnoxious. He knew there was news.

"What's up, Dad. I'm pregnant," I said, quiet and slow.

"What?" he asked.

"I'm pregnant," I said again, this time more clearly.

Dad was silent, no doubt letting the news sink in. But only for a beat. "Praise God," he yelled into the receiver. "Praise God! That's a blessing, baby! I'm coming to take you to breakfast. Let's celebrate!"

No more than a half hour later, he was at my doorstep, grinning and grabbing my hand and tucking me into the front seat of his pickup truck. We ended up at McDonald's; I sat across from him with my pregnant-lady appetite and that big breakfast special—the one with the pancakes, eggs, and sausage. And as I stuffed my face, Daddy spoke good things into me. "Let me tell you something," he said, leaning in. "Hold your head up high. A baby is a blessing. This is going to be your strength right here. It ain't gonna stop you."

He knew like I knew that God doesn't make mistakes and my son was put into my life at that specific moment for a reason. He was right: every moment with my baby in my belly made me stronger and more focused. I was exactly what I told my mother I would be: a happy, fat, pregnant woman who got salty only when she was hungry. I didn't have morning sickness. My hair was thick, beautiful, and long. I got around campus to every one of my classes all winter long, without missing so much as a lecture or an assignment. I didn't consider it hard, it just was what it was. I got acclimated and refused to treat my pregnancy as though it were an obstacle. I was boisterous and in-your-face with it. Of course, there were haters and naysayers sneaking looks at my belly and whispering, "Taraji's pregnant," and praying for my downfall. They thought I would stop. Little did they know, I was just getting started.

The first person I made this clear to was my drama professor Mike Malone. I marched my fat ass right up to him one afternoon and called his name like only I could.

"Oh God," he said, shaking his head and laughing. He always did that when he saw me coming; he used to tell me all the time that I reminded him of my idol, Debbie Allen, with whom he was close. I was a spitfire, he'd say, just like her. "What do you want?"

"Look here: don't you bench me because I'm pregnant," I said through clenched teeth, my belly poking through my T-shirt. "Just because I'm fat doesn't mean anything."

And when auditions came for a play Mr. Malone was directing called *E Man,* I waddled my fat ass in there and sang the hell out of the audition song and did the choreography, big belly and all, and then I leaned into my right hip and looked at him dead in the eye.

Mr. Malone gave me that part, but not out of pity. I earned it. The play was about a man's attributes and all the personalities attached to them, each of which came to life. I played his cheating wife, and Mr. Malone switched up the part a bit so that my pregnancy made sense: under the rewrite, my character was supposed to be pregnant and unsure of whether it was her husband or her side piece who'd fathered the child. I was doing choreography on that stage and climbing up ladders and doing everything a non-pregnant person would have done, so much so that people were convinced that I was wearing a pregnancy pillow to get through it all. "How are you doing that?" they kept asking. "It looks like you're pregnant for real."

"I am," I'd say, and keep right on moving.

Nobody gave me grief after that, because I didn't give anyone a reason to think for even a second that I couldn't handle the work that acting involves, the academics, and the pregnancy. My core group of friends—artsy folk who had nothing but love in their hearts—had my back, and that's all that mattered to me. That's all I ever required—support for my journey.

. . .

I went into labor on Mother's Day, just after Mark took our mothers and me to dinner. I'm at least 95 percent positive I ate my way into the contractions. The whole time I was stuffing my face, Mark was clowning with me like he always did, calling me a beached whale and a few other things that had me cackling and feeling good. I swear, all that teasing is the reason why Marcell came out looking just like his daddy; they've got the same head and eyes, the same thick, hard, leathery hands. Marcell is Mark's boy, indeed. And Mark was so excited to be his father. He was Johnny-on-the-spot when it came time to beat it over to Presbyterian Hospital in Washington, DC, just blocks from Catholic University; it was he who helped me into the wheelchair and rushed me through the halls into the emergency room. My God, he was so excited and nervous, he was bumping me all into the walls. "Calm down, dammit, you're going to make me have the baby right here in this chair!" I yelled after he pushed me right into a wall, too clumsy with excitement to steer the damn thing.

He was equally antsy in the labor and delivery room, as was my entire entourage of family and friends who came to witness my son's birth. Mark alternately celebrated with his boys in the hospital parking lot and in the room with me, where he did everything from read the newspaper to catnap. And when I took to the hallway to walk through the labor pains, he and my parents led the pack. Every time I had a contraction, I would stop and the group would stop, too, and stare at me, and then when the pain subsided and I could see something other than stars, I'd walk again and they would, too. We were causing such a ruckus that at some point, one of the nurses came out and let us have it. "You know there are other people giving birth here," she said, huffing. "You can't have the whole second floor!"

She didn't have any more problems out of us when it came time to push, though. Mark was front and center, with the camera to his eye, aimed at the miracle revealing himself on the delivery table. When Marcell finally made his big debut, Mark lay on top of me and cried tears so joyous, so infectious, everyone else in the room fell out in tears, too. "You gave me a son," he said, in complete euphoria as our baby, wrapped in a bundle of blue just like in my dream, nuzzled against my chest.

It was beautiful, and it stayed that way for a while, too; Mark was an attentive dad in the beginning, picking up and dropping off the baby while I took my classes and went to work, making sure I had what I needed to juggle the demands of both school and my job while parenting a newborn. We were doing exactly what I'd envisioned for us: we were a family, and I was holding us down while helping Mark see that life could be good if we worked together.

But the novelty wore off and life got real again. With his work schedule, my classes, a new baby, and the physical and financial difficulty of juggling it all, tensions ran high in my apartment, which we were now sharing. Finally, his temper started getting the best of him and the closer we became, the more complex things got, the more violent he became. It started with him barking at me when I asked simple questions, and quickly escalated to confrontation when I'd question his whereabouts or why he would show up late picking me up from work. The curses would fly and there would be a grab or two, especially if I called him out on his bullshit. I found myself screaming at him more and more, as his excuses for not being around became more implausible and his accountability less dependable. Just when I thought it couldn't get worse, things escalated.

. . .

I hardly ever questioned his whereabouts. He was a grown man, and I trusted him, so, like a dummy, I believed Mark when he said he was out with the baby or doing odd jobs or looking for work. But on this one particular evening, he had my car and I was late for work on the cruise ship, where I was the supervisor, responsible for making sure everything and everyone ran smoothly. What kind of example would I set as a supervisor by showing up late? I was pacing back and forth, mad as hell, punching Mark's pager number into the house phone and standing over the receiver, cursing as I waited for him to call me back. Marcell, who was about a year old and just learning how to walk, was trying to keep up with my pacing. He was only a baby, but he could sense my distress.

Finally, I heard Mark's key rattling in the front door a good half hour after I was supposed to have punched in at my job. I was undone. "Where the hell you been with my car?" I yelled as he pushed the door open. "You know I had to be at work. You're so damn disrespectful!"

I whooped. He whooped. Then, the next thing I knew, Mark's balled-up fist was coming straight for my face. I fell onto the bed crying and holding my mouth; blood seeped off my lips and across my teeth, washing a nasty, bitter, metallic taste over my tongue. Droplets splashed across my shoes, the dark red slowly creeping into the fibers of my suede boots. Marcell's screams rose into the air, thick and piercing. It was just like the scene from *Baby Boy* in which Yvette finds the condoms in the backseat pocket of her car and confronts Jody about his cheating ways, only to get socked dead in her eye for her troubles. Life imitating art.

I pulled my hand from my mouth and looked at the blood on my trembling fingers. Tears formed in my throat, traveled up to my nose, and finally pooled into my eyes. My words crackled like thunder. "This is over! Get your shit and get out!" I growled as I rushed toward the phone. Mark already was headed to the closet to get his things when I began dialing my father's house; he was crying and snatching the drawers of the bureau open and stuffing his clothes into a bag when my little sister, April, answered the phone. All she heard was her big sister, seventeen years her senior, screaming and crying into the receiver; without my having to articulate a word, she started screaming, too, calling for my father.

"What's wrong, baby?" my father said, terror ringing his words.

"Daddy, I need you!" I yelled.

I didn't have to say anything else. I don't know if he took a jet plane over or if he had a police escort to clear traffic, but I do know this: he was at my door within five minutes of that phone call. April, little squirt with plaits and barrettes and baubles in her hair, burst through the door and made a beeline for her nephew, scooping him up into her arms as she tried to soothe him. She was frantic. By contrast, my father, eerily, was the picture of calm. He walked slowly toward the closet where Mark was packing with his hands in his pockets, and when Mark was in his line of sight, Daddy planted himself on the hardwood floor, towering over my soon-to-be ex, and stared him down.

"You didn't have to put your hands on her," he said, finally, slowly, which surprised me. All my life, after all, Daddy was the one you called only when you were ready to launch the nuclear bomb. You didn't ask for his help with inconsequential things, because when he arrived on the scene, his guns were already blazing and he was taking out everything in sight. Survivors weren't an option. I expected my father to rip Mark from limb to limb. Daddy later told me that despite his newly Christian ways, he'd had a sixth sense that Mark had hit me and had actually plotted a way to kill Mark in the moments it took him to get to my place. "I literally was going to walk in, snap his neck, throw him over the balcony, and call the cops," he said, a sinister look darkening his eyes. "I'd planned on telling the police, 'It was self-defense. Look at my daughter's mouth.' But I prayed to God all the way over here; my grandson was in this room and I couldn't take his father."

Instead, Daddy faced off against the man who'd bloodied his daughter by talking rationally. "I understand it's hard out here for a man," Daddy told Mark. "But you're better than that. This is my daughter you hit. She's a woman. Real men don't do that."

Mark stood there and cried while my father gave him a heart-to-heart speech about how he'd done the same thing to my mother, and how it had ruined his relationship with her and had obliterated his chances of being a full-time father to the love of his life, me. I knew firsthand that this was something my father had long regretted, and over the years, after he cleaned himself up and got himself together and found God, he made a point of apologizing to both my mother and even her husband for laying hands on her.

I didn't want an apology from Mark. Though our relationship had long been rocky, it hadn't been physically abusive until that evening. Still, I knew that if it happened once, it would happen again and again. His punch knocked me into reality; like a dog who tastes bloody meat and never, ever wants to go back to dry kibble, a man who hits his lover once will never go back to keeping his hands to himself in the middle of an argument. I knew that well, especially because I was the product of an abusive relationship. "That's a seed I sowed," my father would say days later, after Mark was gone. "I knew I would pay for what I did to your mother, that it would come back through one of my babies. This is my fault."

It wasn't anyone's fault, and I was no one's victim. We simply couldn't work it out. Like my mother before me, I made the difficult decision to cut off the romantic relationship with the father of my child, not just for my sake, but also for that of my baby boy.

With that separation, my forever man, my first love, was no more, and my dream of building a family with him was over. In so many judgmental eyes, I'd become another statistic: a baby mama. But if one tucks that judgment in a back pocket for even a second and surveys the situation with clear-eyed focus, my becoming a single mother wasn't about being an irresponsible woman with a child; for me, it was about making a sound parenting decision that would ultimately save our lives.

Of course, choosing to be a single mother, even under such dire circumstances, still opened me up to some severe criticism. The common-held assumption used to be that if there's no diamond on the ring finger of the hand pushing the baby stroller, the mother attached to it must be an irresponsible, lazy ass who got pregnant by accident (or on purpose so she could live off the government, depending on who's standing on the Single Moms Suck soapbox), and the poor baby in said stroller is either a mistake, a statistic, or a paycheck. Hardly anyone ever considers that the children of black single mothers are made from love—that we care deeply about our babies and, like any mother with a heart that beats and a mind that is reasonably right, want the very best for them.

Charge that to the national conversation on parenting and motherhood, which has, for the longest time, relegated moms of color and single moms of all races, ethnicities, and backgrounds to the media equivalent of the children's table, where we're all too often told to shut up while the "mainstream" moms who stuck to the rules—"first comes love, then comes marriage, then comes baby in the baby carriage"—have their say on everything from work-life balance and stay-at-home mothering to mundane parenting matters, like teething, potty training, and getting your kid to sleep through the night. The only time anyone cares to hear our take on parenting, it seems, is when the conversation's focus is our pathology: dropout rates, poverty, crime, fatherlessness, the list goes on. Sure, with time, the social ostracism attached to being a single mother has diminished to some extent; chalk that up to the increase in our numbers across race and class lines and the paparazzi lens that stays trained on movie stars and pop singers happily raising their children alone, with neither apology nor guilt. It helps, too, that the celebrity children of single moms make a point of telling the world that their mothers are saints whose hard work, love, dedication, and sacrifices saw them through. Hell, even presidents of the United States—four of them, in fact—were raised by single mothers, a detail that, in the presidential campaign and election of Barack Obama, was a point of pride, rather than a mark against him.

Nevertheless, mention that you're a single mom, and all too many of us still have to cut through a thick, gristly layer of stigma before we're given our proper due. I have to say, I'm consistently amazed at how personally people take it when a black single mom gets some shine for being a good mother to her children sans the ring. Everyone, black people included, reserves a special kind of vitriol for us single moms, calling us and our children out of our names, with absolutely no regard for the fact that we can be as smart, beautiful, and accomplished in our own right and as passionate about our babies and our roles as moms as any married mother. Each of us chose to have our babies. How, exactly, does the choice not to be married to the fathers of our children personally affect our critics? Are they any richer or poorer because of our decisions? Are their kids missing out on something because I didn't marry the father of my child? Is the earth about to spin off its rotational axis because my household mirrors the households of more than 70 percent of black households in which children are being raised by a single parent? What I'm sure of is this: The grace and understanding for the familial choices of married women is a given. The humanity of single moms comes with asterisks, ridicule, and judgmental questions.

So I'll set my personal record straight: my baby, Marcell Johnson, was most certainly the product of a loving relationship. Yes, it was dysfunctional, sure; his father and I were young, dumb, and clueless about how to make our partnership work. But we did love one another and were in love when I got pregnant with our son. Though Mark and I weren't actively trying to have a baby together, Marcell is not a mistake. He was—and always will be—wanted.

I never saw my baby as a roadblock to my goals or a strike against my ability to do exactly what I planned to do with my life; I simply started planning and dreaming about ways I would get what I wanted out of life *while* I had a baby on my hip. Having my son gave me a laser-sharp focus. That is the miracle of single motherhood: it is not easy to raise a human being *with* a partner, but doing so alone requires a herculean effort that is all muscle and grit and sacrifice, built up with repetitive sets of sacrifice. Whatever you gain, whatever you earn, you give to your baby and you work triple hard to show your child—not anyone else—that moving forward, no matter how tiny the steps, is possible. This is a single mother's love.

Destined to be on TV, age two.

Daddy Boris and me.

Santa and me.

"Styling" pigtails.

Mom Bernice and me.

Wearing another great hairdo.

Rocking my mushroom hair.

Posing for a selfie with Dad.

Holding up the Eiffel Tower in Paris, France. (Courtesy of Ashunta Sheriff)

Walking down the streets of Paris in my slippers. (Courtesy of Ashunta Sheriff)

Marcel and me.

Taking pictures with Alexander Wang before leaving for the Met Gala 2015. (Courtesy of Ashunta Sheriff)

Family at Christmas.

7

Going to Hollywood

I simply could not juggle caring for a newborn, finishing up my senior-year classes, and working, so something had to go. It couldn't be my kid or my education, the one thing I was sure was going to open doors for me and, by extension, my baby. So I went to the social services office and struggled through the nastiness and contempt the social workers threw my way so that I could get the food stamps, rent subsidy, and baby items I needed to keep us fed and housed while I did what I had to do to graduate. I was not ashamed of this, not even for a second: I'd been working since age fourteen and, since age sixteen, paying taxes into the system, which was designed, in part, specifically to help families like mine sustain themselves while they did what they had to do to get back on their feet. Public assistance gave me the support my family needed. Sure enough I graduated—I walked across that stage that fine day in May 1995 in my cap and gown with Marcell in my arms to collect my bachelor's degree in fine arts. Shortly after that fateful fight with Mark, I gave up my apartment in DC and moved into my father's home in Clinton, Maryland, to save money on rent and continued to work on the crew of the *Odyssey*.

Now, even with the monumental education I got at Howard, it took me some time to pursue my passion. I still had big dreams of being a star, but reality deferred them. I was a single mother with a baby to support on my own and bills that weren't going to pay themselves. I was pulling shifts and making enough money to get back on my feet again, and eventually I would stack enough cash to buy myself a little town house somewhere down the line and live a decent life raising my son. So focused was I on getting money and keeping up with my responsibilities that I actually lost focus on the bigger prize: acting took a backseat to the real-life hustle of single parenthood.

My father, who always saw bigger things for me, even when I didn't immediately see them for myself, wanted me to have so much more. It was he who tapped me on the shoulder one day, pulled my face toward his, and ordered me to stop hustling backward. "What are you still doing here in Maryland?" he asked me one day while I sat at the kitchen table feeding Marcell. I was in my work clothes, ready to rush out for the evening shift, with an exclusive focus on squaring my baby away before I hit the door.

"What do you mean?" I asked. "I got a job."

"Yeah, yeah," he said, waving his hand dismissively. "But didn't you graduate with a degree in acting? Ain't no acting jobs in Maryland. How you expect to catch fish on dry land?"

I looked at him, alternately confused and a tad annoyed by the conversation, considering I had only a few more minutes before I needed to be on the other side of town. I absentmindedly looked at my watch, then focused on putting the last spoon of mashed potatoes and peas in my baby's mouth. Daddy was undeterred. "You gotta go where the fish are," he said, this time more urgently.

"What you talking about? Fish?" I asked, even more annoyed.

"The jobs! You gotta go where the jobs are! Los Angeles!" he said, exasperated. "You want acting jobs, but they're not here in Maryland, they're in Los Angeles. Where your cousins are."

He wasn't lying. At the time, my cousin Dee was in Los Angeles with her son, Bobby, who, inspired by my star turns at Howard, had become a child actor and rapper. Little Bobby would always come to see me in my plays, with his little lemon head perched on a seat right on the front row, feet all dangling and swinging above the floor. When I hit the stage, I would have to focus above his head because he would be sitting there, staring up, beaming at me, smitten and totally turned out by my acting—quite the sweet little distraction when I was trying to stay in character, but a distraction nonetheless. Still, he got enough of the acting bug to get good—good enough for a Maryland-based manager, Linda Townsend of Linda Townsend Management, to send him on an audition in Los Angeles, where he booked a gig on a UPN show called *Minor Adjustments,* starring fellow Howard University alum Wendy Raquel Robinson. Unbeknownst to me, Dad already had put in a call to Dee, seeing if she would be open to me moving into the two-bedroom apartment she and Bobby were staying in while the show's season played out. She was on board. "I'm going to send her out there with you, then," Dad told Dee.

My father had a gift for putting an idea in your head and making you think you came up with it. Before I knew it, I was chucking up deuces to that comfortable life in Maryland and making plans to throw myself into the mix of the cutthroat entertainment industry. At the time, I was a twenty-six-year-old single mother—born and raised in the heart of Chocolate City with very little professional acting experience on my résumé, zero prospects for acting work, and very few leads that could get me in the room with the people who could get me auditions and jobs. In other words, to anyone even remotely familiar with Hollywood and its inner workings, I would have been tagged easily with the "least likely to succeed" stamp across my forehead. But none of that mattered to me or my father or most anyone else who loved and wanted more for me.

Within days of my father putting that bug in my ear, I was considering where I'd go to pursue my acting career. Today, with film productions opening up work for actors and crews in non-traditional film cities like New Orleans, Atlanta, Cleveland, Chicago, and the like, there are plenty of places an actress trying to lay down roots can go to find work and a decent living, but back when I was first getting started, there really were only two places for working actors: New York for the theater scene and Los Angeles for film and television. After some careful consideration, I nixed New York, because theater doesn't pay, the rent is too damn high, and finding affordable child care would have been about as doable as catching a first-class flight to Pluto. Besides, I was checking for Cali because I was seeing fellow Bisons on television: at that time, Wendy Raquel Robinson, Paula Jai Parker, Anthony Anderson, Isaiah Washington, and Marlon Wayans were just a few of the Howard alums who were making a name for themselves on both the small and big screens, and all of us who'd graduated alongside and after them were watching and marveling at their success. So I decided. "You're right, Dad. California it is."

A few months later, I made it to California on a buddy pass I bought for one hundred dollars from a friend of mine who worked for an airline, with a mere seven hundred dollars to my name and baby Marcell on my hip. Though I was being managed by Linda Townsend back in Maryland, I did not have an agent. I did not have a place of my own. I did not have a car. I did not have a job. I did not have a SAG card, which would allow me to actually work as an actress. But I was the ultimate hustler, and by hook or crook, I was going to be a star.

Within days of landing at Los Angeles International Airport and dropping off my suitcases at Dee's place, I hit the ground running, signing up with a temp agency and nailing down a job at an accounting firm. I promptly made myself completely indispensable so that I could make the argument for why they should make me semipermanent rather than send me back to the temp agency, which would have farmed me out all over the sprawling city at all hours of the day and night. I had a baby and needed stability—a steady job with steady hours at the same place each and every day so that I knew where I'd be, what time I could get back home to my child, and when I'd be able to audition. In addition to working my tail off and making myself indispensable, I played the single mom card to get what I needed from the office manager. That single mother card is *real*—you better understand and respect that. "Look," I said, "I got a little baby and he needs his mother. I'm a hard worker, I promise you that, but for the sake of my baby, I need to have a schedule—some consistency. I can't be sent to Woodland Hills one day and to Beverly Hills on another. I need to be stationed at this office with regular hours so I can get home to my son."

The office manager cheerfully accepted my proposal.

"I came here to be an actress," I said matter-of-factly as I grabbed a pen from her desk and leaned into the paperwork she'd asked me to sign. "I'm telling you this so that you know I'm going to need time to audition and work when I book gigs."

She smirked when I said that. I'll never forget that look—the curl of the lip, the narrowed side-eye, that huff of air that she pushed up from her gut and through her thin nostrils. I'd seen it before. It was that same dismissive "yeah, right" look I got from a few of my classmates when I declared I could both be a mother and graduate college on time. It was the look on those social workers' faces when I told them I'd be on my feet soon enough. It was on the faces of a few folks, too, when I announced I was leaving everyone I loved and all that I knew to move to Hollywood in pursuit of an acting career. Though I was used to those smirks, they always rubbed me the wrong way, and I never forgot them. But rather than discourage me, they were like gallons of high-grade gasoline adding fuel to my fire. I have faith in God, and I know my purpose, so I have no need to be nasty about it when someone doubts me. I simply put my head down and work hard while I wait for the tides to turn in my favor; that's when my actions and my blessings speak volumes. My office manager wasn't a believer, but I'd gotten out of her exactly what I wanted—a steady paycheck at a job that afforded me steady hours.

When I collected my first check, I stacked it with the seven hundred dollars I'd brought with me to Los Angeles, and with the help of my cousin Dee, we started ticking off the list of things I needed to set up camp in Los Angeles. First up was buying myself a used car. Dee kicked in some cash and took me over to the airport, where they were holding car auctions, and helped me scoop up an old Nissan Sentra. That thing was gray and dingy with a front driver's seat belt that *tied* over my lap, but I put Marcell's old car seat in the back and I drove all over Hollywood in that bad boy, without a care in the world how it measured up to the more flashy cars in the ever-glamorous Tinseltown. I didn't have one problem showing up for auditions in my Nissan, with Marcell's car seat, littered with Cheerios, goldfish crackers, and toys, filling up the backseat, and parking between a Benz and a Porsche.

I hustled my way into an apartment, too. I didn't dally while looking for this place, because my cousin's show was about to wrap up and Dee was heading back to DC, so time was ticking. Plus, my credit was horrible, I wasn't making much money—about ten dollars an hour at the accounting firm—and I needed to get in front of a property manager whom I could convince to rent to me, even though my TransUnion and Equifax reports were shining a harsh fluorescent light on the late credit card balances I was struggling to pay off while attending college and caring for a new baby. In other words, a bitch couldn't really afford to be choosy. Almost as quickly as I started looking, I found a potential spot for Marcell and me, a cute little studio apartment in a green garden building surrounded by palm trees. "Oooh! This is so California!" I exclaimed when I saw it.

I put on the best performance of my life to get the property manager, a sweet little old black lady, to overlook all my financial issues and rent me that studio. My award-worthy persuasion involved tears. I cried *real tears* for that place. "I won't be late on my rent," I said, water welling in my eyes. "I'll keep my place spotless, I won't make any noise or have any wild parties, no strangers coming in and out of the property." Then I went in for the kill, taking a breath and turning on the full waterworks. "Please, I just got here and I'm trying really hard to better my life. I need this place for me and my baby."

She had a heart and gave me the keys to the apartment, for which I was so grateful. But when I unpacked my suitcases and said good-bye to my cousin and I closed the door behind her and sat down on my chair with my baby in my lap, something just didn't set right with me. Perhaps I was experiencing a little bit of postpartum depression. I was a new mother with a one-year-old, sitting in a little-ass studio all alone, my support system—my parents, my friends, my rocks—thousands of miles away on the other side of the country. Perhaps I was upset that the studio apartment, though mine, didn't stand up to even the bare-minimum lifestyle I'd promised to build for my son. When I found out I was pregnant, every night my prayer for my baby and me was that God would allow me to provide for my son exactly what my mother had provided for me. I always had my own bedroom; we always had a car; we always had food on the table, and the lights were always on; we never had to move from place to place and were never put out. Luxuries were scant, but we had the basics. Still, something else was speaking to me. Call it a mother's intuition.

Turns out my instincts were right.

It was a coworker who inadvertently let me know that I was living in one of the sketchiest buildings in one of Hollywood's sketchiest neighborhoods. I was in the break room with him, unpacking my lunch, when I asked, quite innocently, "Where's the hood around here? I haven't really seen the projects. What do they look like? Where I'm from, they're high-rises."

"You know the little garden apartments? The ones that look like motels?" he asked between sips of his coffee. "Those are low-income housing."

"What? Really?" I asked, stunned. He was describing exactly where I lived. In the hood!

I took off my rose-colored glasses and started paying attention from that moment on. One evening I arrived home late with Marcell bundled in my arms, just in time to witness a little two-year-old girl wandering around outside in the courtyard looking lost, her hair unkempt, her clothes disheveled. I stopped in my tracks and watched her in wonder, alternately concerned she was going to hurt herself or someone was going to snatch her, and curious, too, about why, exactly, a toddler was teetering around in the dark by herself. Then a piercing scream filled the air, startling me. "You trifling bitch, come get your daughter," a Latino woman yelled from the balcony of her apartment, a few flights up.

Another woman, this one white, snatched open her door; a black man, partially undressed, was standing just beyond her, as she leaned over the rail, calling out to her baby. I don't know if she was a whore or getting high off crack or what her deal was, but it sure put me on edge. A few days later, again when I was arriving home late with my baby in my arms, I spotted a guy stalking around, looking like a total pedophile. "That's it," I mumbled under my breath as I jiggled the key in my door. "I gotta get out of here. I can't do this anymore." My baby and I were on the move.

I'd visited my friend and fellow Howard alum Jemal McNeil at his place in what is now known as Silver Lake, and really liked where he was living; it was an apartment in a cluster of bungalows overlooking a private courtyard. It was very family oriented; the landlord and her husband lived downstairs in a one-bedroom, and another single mother lived in the other two-bedroom with her son, who also happened to be Marcell's age. As fate would have it, the two-bedroom just above Jemal was available; the landlord's mother had lived there before she died, and her son, who inherited the property, couldn't bring himself to rent it out. The place was exactly as the mother had left it: old, with a granny apple–green shaggy carpet and odd colors on the wall. But it was just perfect for Marcell and me. I cried my way out of my lease at the hood spot—all that landlord knew was that I had a family emergency and I needed to get away—then got my little change together and my performance face on and told the new landlord my story. I left there with the keys to my new place and a five-hundred-dollar-per-month lease. I had just enough money to replace the ratty shag carpet with some of that cheap, thin, gray carpet that buildings use in their offices. It wasn't much, but it had exactly what I needed: a parking spot, a bedroom for my child, a friend downstairs who made it so that I felt safe, a familylike atmosphere with a fellow single mom whose son got along with my baby, a day care just down the street for Marcell, and a landlord who trusted I was going to do what I promised I would do. It wasn't the most luxurious spot in the world, but this time, it felt right.

"Okay," I said, sitting down in my living room, peering into Marcell's eyes. "Now we can build." In that moment, I couldn't help but think that this was how my mother must have felt when she got her first apartment when I was a young girl.

Build is what I did. With a safe place to stay, a car, and a job, I could work on my purpose: to become a big-time, paid, SAG-card-carrying actress in the city where stars are made. My manager from back home, Linda Townsend, put me in touch with an agency whose sole direction was to get me the gigs I needed to score that SAG card. I needed to book three roles as an extra, plus pay the $1,100 fee to join the union. Two of those extra roles came at my cousin's job on *Minor Adjustments*. It was a relatively easy gig—nothing like the non-SAG hustle I had to pull on *Malcolm X*—because my cousin took good care of me, letting me chill in his dressing room and eat with him and his mom. The third role came when I worked as an extra on *3rd Rock From the Sun,* a sitcom on which my DC homegirl Simbi Khali was working. Simbi, an alum of the Duke Ellington School of the Arts, was an inspiration because she, too, had left DC and was doing exactly what I wanted to do: making it in Hollywood. Every time I was around Simbi, she would talk about the process—what it took to secure roles, how to hone my craft, what events I should be sure to attend, the people I needed to know—and I absorbed it like a sponge. I'm grateful to her for that.

With her help, I became SAG eligible. And every time I would book a job after that, I would chip away at that union fee until finally it was official: I was a card-carrying member of the Screen Actors Guild. I was on my way to my blessing—exactly what God intended for me, and everything I'd hustled practically all my life to be: a working actress. This single mother was on a mission not only to make that dream a reality, but also to be the finest example of a success story for my son—to let him know that when I whispered in his ear, "You can be anything, baby," I wasn't bullshitting. This, my story, is proof positive of that.

8

Raising a Black Boy

My mother swears all the singing and dancing I did at Howard University when I was pregnant with Marcell made my baby push his way into this world with a heart full of joy. I can't say I disagree with her. Marcell was the cutest, jolliest baby ever. He never cried, was never sick, and was always laughing—a bundle of dimples and giggles with the pull of a magnet. My study group would show up to my apartment to go over lessons and scenes together and they'd barely say hello to me at my front door before they rushed in looking for my Marcell. There he'd be, tucked in his crib with John Coltrane's *A Love Supreme* floating from my boom box's speakers, staring up at the gaggle of smiling faces cooing his way; he'd stick out his tongue, wave his little arms and legs in the air, and flash that mouthful of gums, and my classmates' hearts would do Alvin Ailey–worthy leaps across the room. The same was true when I'd take Marcell's little hand in mine and walk with him through the mall or the grocery store. There he'd be, this sweet, bubbly little three-year-old, toddling by my side; he'd barely keep time with my stride as we tried to get some shopping done, only to be stopped every ten feet or so to let a crowd of strangers ooh and ah over my adorable baby. He was a rock star, my kid. The whole world loves a sweet little chubby brown boy.

Until they don't. When they get some length on those legs and those baby curls morph into a mass of naps, suddenly everything is new. Where once admirers saw cuteness, there is only threatening stereotype, and all that brightness that made those adorable little black boys irresistible is overshadowed by the dark cloud of assumptions, disdain, and, yes, racism. This is neither speculation nor conjecture from an overly sensitive mom; it is verifiable, indisputable fact. Just a few years ago, headlines blared with news of three different studies that showed that black boys as young as ten are mistaken as more than four years older, are more likely to face police violence if accused of a crime, and are often denied the assumption of innocence typically afforded children when they act like, well, children. It is how Tamir Rice, a baby-faced twelve-year-old kid playing shoot-'em-up games with a toy gun, can get gunned down by police within literally seconds of their arriving on the scene, with the shooting officer saying he thought the boy looked like a twenty-year-old. It is how Trayvon Martin's killer can get away with claiming a skinny kid wearing a hoodie in the rain, with Skittles and iced tea in his pockets, was a threat. It is how a fourteen-year-old Emmett Till could end up at the bottom of the Tallahatchie River, beaten, broken, gouged, and tied with barbed wire to a cotton gin fan, and his killers could not only be acquitted of his murder, but go on to brag about how that child "got what he deserved," without any legal repercussion. In other words, our babies—our sons—get buried in an avalanche of low expectations, negative perceptions, oft-quoted statistics, and outright danger that denies them their basic humanity. And it is hard as hell, as a mother of a black male, to stand there with your baby in your arms, watching the clouds form and the sky turn gray—hearing that rumbling thunder, knowing that an immense, intense, never-ending storm of criticism, judgment, and outright abuse is about to rain down on your son's head.

For Marcell, it began as early as kindergarten, before he'd barely opened his first pack of crayons—before, even, he could write his own name. It happened right after school, when the sun is high and the kids are restless from a long day's work and the teacher opens the door and shoos her young charges outside to let off a little steam before pickup. From what I gathered from the story, a few kids from his class were jumping around, plotting out a game of hide-and-seek, when Marcell tried to join in on the fun. "Can I play?" he asked.

One of his classmates was quick to answer: "No," he said, without even a moment of hesitation.

"Why?" Marcell asked.

"Because you're black," he said.

Confused and upset that he'd been barred from playing, Marcell tucked himself away in a quiet corner of the play area until I arrived to pick him up. I could tell by the way his shoulders were hunched over that something wasn't right. "Hey, baby, give me some sugar," I said, waiting with outstretched arms for my afternoon greeting. "How was your day? What's wrong?"

"They said I couldn't play with them," Marcell offered in the most pitiful little baby voice I'd ever heard.

"What?" I asked, my happy-to-see-you face quickly morphing into a furrowed brow. "What happened that they said you couldn't play with them?"

"He said it's because I'm black," Marcell said, just as pitiful as could be. "But I don't understand, Mommy, because my shirt is green, my pants are blue, and my sneakers are white."

"He said what to you? Who said it? Show me," I demanded.

Marcell pointed in the direction of the cubbies; at the end of the tip of his little finger was the boy, a Middle Eastern kid with a thick accent and skin as brown, if not more so, than Marcell's, and his mom, who was helping him gather his things. "Wait right here," I told Marcell. "Don't you move."

I caught her in the parking lot, tucking her son into his car seat. "Hey, let me speak to you for a minute," I said. I'm sure the fury in my eyes was the impetus for her to close the car door before she gave me her full attention. I let her have that, then confronted her head-on. "How dare you!" I snarled. "What are you teaching your son at home that he's bold enough to say something so foul to my son?"

"I don't understand," she said. "What did he do? What is going on?"

"Your son told my son that he couldn't play with him because he's black," I said, seething. "What are you teaching your child at home? Because I know this is not his fault. He's a five-year-old child. That's the kind of mess that gets taught to kids at home." She raised her palms in surrender, trying to interject, but I wasn't

about to let her have at it. I was too disgusted to entertain explana-
tions and excuses. "My son would never say something like that.
He's being taught to love and respect all people, no matter their
color, and what I will not stand for is for some child to refuse to
give him the same respect on the playground. How's your son
going to make my son feel left out anyway? They got the same
color skin!"

I can't even begin to recount what she said back because I
didn't give a damn about the words coming out of her mouth.
I just wanted to make clear that there would be some hell in the
city if her kid ever spoke to my kid like that again.

Later, after we got home and unpacked his book bag and had
a snack, I sat Marcell down and tried to explain to him in black
and white the complicated Technicolor of race. "Baby, you're
cute right now and the world loves you, but when you get bigger
you're going to become a threat."

"What do you mean, Mommy?" he asked, all that innocence
shining like halo light around his head.

"Well, there are people in this world who do not like other
people because they're black. And that's an awful thing because
skin color shouldn't matter, baby. We like anybody who has a
good heart, and it's a good thing to let them play hide-and-seek
with you, no matter their color."

Marcell looked down at his hands and arms and then back at
me, seemingly more confused than he was before our talk. "But
my skin is brown, Mommy."

"And it's beautiful, baby," I said, shaking my head and giving
him a warm smile. "Your skin is brown and beautiful."

· · ·

To this day, even as a twentysomething young black man who has felt the sting of racism and witnessed firsthand its effects on how we relate to one another as humans, Marcell still can't wrap his mind around someone hating him because of the color of his skin. It really messes with his mind because he's spent his lifetime surrounded by a virtual United Nations of friends from different racial, cultural, and socioeconomic backgrounds and has always embraced them for who they are, what they're interested in, and whether they have an intimate human-to-human connection, rather than what they look like. Indeed, his best friend growing up was a French boy named Anton, whom he adored not because of his skin color or background, but because they liked the same things: video games and climbing trees in the backyard and riding bicycles with the wind whipping in their faces. This is Marcell's way. The way it should be.

We mothers, the ones charged with the care and upkeep of black boys, know the score. Black single moms are constantly beat up for our choice to have our children, but it is our boys who feel the impact of that blunt force. The blows come wrapped in a sledgehammer of statistics and pathology, with society tying our sons' skin color and the marital status of their mothers to a heavy weight of low expectations. It seems as though everybody is standing around waiting for our boys to prove that black boys, especially those raised by single moms, have a propensity for violence, are probable criminals, lack education, are more likely to take illicit drugs, and are more likely to suffer from mental disorders— and on and on. From the moment the doctor smacked Marcell's butt and said, "It's a boy," I knew I had to come primed and ready for the fight. I was never scared of the prospects—never bowed to the fear that comes with raising a black son in a society that is prone to think the worst, rather than the best, of him. Instead, I steeled myself for the challenge, with this one true mantra: "I'm going to raise a helluva black boy." That's the armor I carried with me—the determination to prove every last one of those statistics wrong. I was blocking bullets aimed at my son's abilities and character early and often. Like the time when his third-grade teacher suggested I put him on medication because she thought he was too hyper in class. I saw nothing wrong; as far as I was concerned, my son's behavior was no different from any other creative, inquisitive, and energetic eight-year-old boy who would much rather jump around and be stimulated than be confined to the same seat for hours on end, stuck in the muck of long, boring lectures and tedious assignments that felt more like busywork than actual learning. When she mentioned attention deficit disorder and slow-tracking my kid, I gave myself two choices: either choke her out or pull my son out of the school. Thankfully for her, I chose the latter.

Near the end of eighth grade Marcell learned firsthand how his skin color made some people unfairly perceive him as hostile. That happened when he was called into the office for throwing down a Ping-Pong paddle in a fit of anger over losing a match. The paddle popped up and accidentally hit a fellow classmate. Granted, Marcell did start to have a little temper around that time, but it was the product of adolescence and hormones, added to which was an undercurrent of hostility he was facing from his teachers and especially his peers, not some kind of academic or emotional deficiency. He had kids calling him the N-word, walking up to him and addressing him in Ebonics—"Yo, yo, yo, Marcell, what up!"—as if my son didn't have a command over the English language, and even asking him, conspiratorially, if he ate fried chicken and drank grape Kool-Aid.

"What are you even talking about?" Marcell would snap. "My mother doesn't cook fried chicken; it's high in cholesterol and it'll kill you. And I've never had Kool-Aid in my life."

Unbeknownst to me, he was dealing with this day in and day out at that school, though I wouldn't find out until years later. Only then did I understand that this kind of attitude was why he wanted to leave one particular school. When he was in the thick of it, however, he would simply tell me he didn't like the school, which, to my ears, translated into "I don't like school."

"Boy, just focus and get your head in them books," I would say, dismissing his complaints. "You can do this." Frankly, I wanted the school to work; as an institution, it was academically sound, plus he had solid connections there, including a pair of Armenian brothers he really liked to hang out with, and Ian, the son of my fellow actress Regina King, whom he counted as a good friend. I thought he was doing just fine.

Then I got that phone call from the teacher that would make me understand just what kind of danger my son was in.

"He was a preemie, so that might have something to do with his abilities," the teacher said nonchalantly one afternoon when I was called up to the school to talk about Marcell's yearly assessment. She actually suggested that my son wouldn't be able to test into a high-performing private high school and proposed that rather than let him graduate, I should approve leaving him back a year at her school. "If we keep him back a year, he can catch up."

"Well, is he failing?" I asked, my forehead pulsing with anger. I knew the answer, and whatever she was going to say didn't matter; I was too disgusted to bother hearing and digesting the words. I just wanted to see her fix her mouth to give me her reasoning for holding back a child who was passing all his classes. The very second sound came out of her mouth, I cut her off. "You know what? It doesn't even matter what you say to me right now. I'll be taking my son out of this school," I said.

"Oh? What school do you have in mind for him, if you don't mind my asking?"

I ticked off a list of considerations and mentioned a private school that was looking to up its diversity and had a new coach who was recruiting players for the school's basketball team. One of my closest friends in the business, Lisa Vidal, who plays Kara on the hit BET show *Being Mary Jane,* had nothing but good things to say about the school. That's where Marcell would go next—somewhere where he was wanted.

"Really," she said smugly, more like a statement than a question. "Well, I don't know if that would be a good fit. He might not be up to the rigorous academic standards they have there." That's when I gathered up my purse and my jacket and pushed back my chair. I needed to get out of there before I caught a case.

That incident and the school's handling of it would be the dawn of my son's racial awakening—when he would realize that skin color and the way society views it, particularly when it comes to black boys, is nuanced, layered, messy, and at times traumatic. I know figuring this out for myself was a devastating

shock, particularly after growing up in a primarily black neighborhood and never having to experience this kind of in-your-face
racism. Southeast DC had its issues, of course, but not the kind
of racial intolerance that would have been immediately apparent
to a sheltered African American girl surrounded by black people
during the week and well-meaning white folk at my weekend extracurricular activities. I didn't get a dose of blatant racism until
freshman year at North Carolina A&T, when my friends and I
got caught up in a massive riot during Greekfest on Labor Day
weekend in Virginia Beach.

The incident made national news, with media accounts blam-
ing the mostly black crowd of vacationing college students for
the violence and property damage that rocked the small beach
community during that fateful holiday weekend in 1989. But
what the stories mostly ignored was the ill treatment we students
faced from the moment we stepped foot on the Virginia Beach
shores—how the hotels raised the rates and imposed minimum
stays to discourage black students from staying at their establish-
ments, how the city passed strict laws barring loud music, jay-
walking, and other things students tend to do while on college
break, how local retailers wouldn't allow more than two or three
black people at a time in their stores, out of fear that we'd steal
something. Even the National Guard had been put on standby
in anticipation of some mess going down, and state police were
patrolling the streets on horses, armed with guns and attitudes.
Plus, rumors that the Ku Klux Klan would work with them to
"keep order" pulsed through the crowds, putting us all on edge.
As far as we students were concerned, the Virginia Beach locals
were doing everything they could to make us feel unwelcomed,

even though we weren't doing anything more egregious than that which white college students do when they're ripping and running on the beaches at Daytona, Panama City, and Fort Lauderdale. And we all felt some kind of way about this.

None of this, of course, stopped us from having a good time. The annual Greekfest was always an incredible weekend of frivolity, fueled by music, partying, and camaraderie, cloaked in unapologetic blackness. Tens of thousands of college-age folks would show up each year for a long weekend's worth of mingling, networking, and, yes, bacchanalia. When I arrived with my friends Pam and Lisa, Virginia Beach was practically vibrating; everywhere our eyes could see, there were cute guys rocking their fraternity colors and blasting music from their cars, and pretty girls in their bikinis and pum pum shorts, sipping their wine coolers, flirting with the frat boys, and dancing and laughing in the streets. It was just healthy, clean, red-blooded American fun among mostly college students and our college-age friends who didn't necessarily go to school but were decent people and liked to have a good time.

Now, as we had our fun, we tried to ignore the poor treatment and excessive rules the city and its residents were imposing, but there was an undercurrent of anger waiting to explode as the police pushed everyone's buttons. Where there was joy, there were, too, pockets of protest and anger, prodded by what we perceived to be police mistreatment. People were being slapped with $500 citations for walking across the street outside of the crosswalk, and cops were using their batons to tap intimidatingly on car windows and angrily ordering drivers to lower their music. The police officers on those horses, their hands on their guns, their eyes hidden behind big mirrored glasses, gave me chills. I could feel the danger in the air. Sure enough, all hell broke loose on Sunday afternoon, and Pam, Lisa, and I were right there when the powder keg exploded.

It started when a guy driving his fancy 300Z down the strip stopped his car in the middle of the street, popped his trunk, and turned up his music, right there where my friends and I were standing, taking in the action and making plans for which party we'd attend later that evening. Using my hand to shield my eyes from the sun, I peeked over at the car to see who was turning up; recognizing him from an encounter a day earlier, I sucked my teeth and shook my head. He was this hustler—some dude with a fake accent and hazel contacts who clearly thought his British cockney and light eyes would earn him favor with the ladies. For the most part, he got it, too, but not with me. He looked like one of those DC-hustling good-for-nothings who didn't mean anyone any good. I didn't trust him or the scene he was drawing. Still, the music—a Boogie Down Productions tune—got everybody hyped, and within moments, black folk were surrounding his car, dancing and laughing and rapping along with the song in the middle of the street and all on the sidewalk. This made one particular shop owner, whose store was being blocked, feel some kind of way—enough so that he came out and started yelling at everybody. One guy in particular got into a screaming match with the store owner, the two of them exchanging expletives and practically spitting in each other's mouths as their faces bulged with anger. I watched as they argued, but out of the corner of my eye, I saw another huge commotion down an alleyway not too far from where we were. I turned toward it just in time to see cops dressed in riot gear, jumping off the helicopter ladder and swarming toward us. They were holding Plexiglas shields over their bodies; their rifles bounced in time to the pounding of their boots on the pavement. The entire scene was surreal—and the scariest mess I'd ever seen.

I squeezed Pam's arm. Nothing had happened to justify their presence—there was no fist-fighting, no one was brandishing weapons or, as far as we knew, getting hurt. We were just a bunch of kids dancing. But here were the police, dressed for war. "Something is about to pop off," I said, shaking my head. "This doesn't feel right."

Just as I said that, someone in the crowd said, "Fuck you! Kick it in, Mookie!" a reference, no doubt, to the scene in Spike Lee's *Do the Right Thing* where Spike's character, Mookie, upset with the choking death of his friend, Radio Raheem, throws a trash can into the glass plate window of the local pizzeria, igniting a huge riot in the streets of Brooklyn. Before anyone had a chance to react, the guy who'd been arguing with the store owner threw something at the shop, and then there was chaos. Fists flew, bodies were tossed, police batons were raising in the air; people were screaming and falling to the ground and running and ducking into the crevices of the storefronts, desperate to escape the melee—the danger. It was like a war zone.

My girlfriends and I took off in the direction of our hotel. We just turned and ran. Pam, poor thing, slammed straight into a bench; she yelped in pain as Lisa and I grabbed her arms and pulled her toward the boardwalk, away from the bedlam. We ran all the way to the opposite end of the beach, as hard as we could. To this day, Pam has that bench imprint on her chest—a physical reminder of what we'll never, ever forget: the day it was made clear to us that, in the eyes of all too many, our blackness relegates us to second-class citizenship.

That incident sent me on a discovery for my blackness. Already, I had been proud of who I am and where I came from—my family, my friends, my community. But that incident at Greek-fest made me dig deeper, to revel in the teachings of Martin, Malcolm, and Garvey, the writings of Baldwin and Ellison, the history of black women in the movement for civil rights and gender parity. I was like a sponge in my unearthing—every book and essay and speech seeping deep into my soul and fine-tuning my voice. I'm proud to be a woman, but specifically I'm proud to be a black woman. The strength, endurance, and legacy of my people mean something to me.

After my son's encounter at his school, blackness meant something to him, too. He went on his own discovery, deep-diving into books, scouring the Internet, watching documentaries, giving himself a clear picture of our history and his place in it. And while he was fact finding, I was talking to him, giving him lessons on how to handle himself when faced with racism, both subtle and brash. "Say 'yes sir' and 'no sir' if you're stopped by the cops, Marcell. No popping off at the mouth," I would tell him. And, "When these knuckleheads out here call you 'nigger,' don't give them the power over you. Just tell them they're the ignorant ones. You know what you are to them? A threat. Because you're intelligent, you're athletic, you stay in those books, and you keep winning. It's killing them that you can come from all this adversity—no daddy, for a while there, no money—and you still winning. You have the power. You have that connection to God. Walk in that, and don't let anyone break your stride."

My lessons sunk in, too; I got to see that up close when he went to his new high school. Though children of color were scant at this particular private institution, the administration really looked out for my son and went out of its way to give him the social and emotional support he needed for academic success. Still, there were a few students who lived in a bubble that kept their interactions with African Americans and other people of color severely limited, leaving my son vulnerable to their ignorance. For instance, one afternoon, an Asian kid with his own ridiculously racist notions about Marcell, got into an argument with my son, and every time he would say something stereotypical and dumb, Marcell, with his slick mouth, would answer him right back with a dis of his own. What can I say? He gets it from his mama. At any rate, the kid, unable to get a rise out of Marcell with his insults, finally resorted to calling my son "nigger." Marcell's response made the Asian kid physically attack him. When Marcell raised his arms and pushed him to protect himself and then stood up out of his chair to get away, his opponent fell to the floor, which made it look like Marcell, a black boy, was standing over another kid after a fistfight.

I got the dean's phone call while I was in New York, filming. I tapped my foot in nervous anger as she recounted what happened. I was waiting for her to drop the bomb; I just knew she was going to kick my son out of that school and I'd be stuck scrambling to find quality education for him while I was, literally, on the other side of the country, working hard to keep that school tuition paid and keep the lights on at home. The shoe never dropped, though. Instead, the dean called to tell me she knew what happened and my son had her full support.

"When the other student called Marcell the N-word, your son said, 'You know the word "nigger" doesn't mean "black," right? It means you're ignorant. So who's the nigger?'" the dean recounted. "If anything, it made the other kid look bad. I'm proud of him for keeping his cool. The N-word isn't a trigger for him, and that's a good thing. That speaks a lot to his character, and says a lot about what a great mother you are."

• • •

My son and I are not perfect—by any stretch. Like any parent and child's dynamic, ours was complicated. The fact of the matter is, as hard as I tried to be the kind of provider who could keep his life as stable as humanly possible, there were some things I simply couldn't provide for a boychild who was missing that critical male presence boys need, who craved a father's love and attention.

For one, the logistics of raising a boy alone were complicated. Showing him how to pee standing up: challenge. Explaining wet dreams: challenge. Giving tips on shaving, butt funk, and condoms: a test for the ages. Illuminating him on the inner-workings of menstruation—at age six!—was a treat. I'll never forget the day he entered the bathroom without knocking, only to discover me in the middle of changing my pad. He almost passed out. "Calm down, boy," I snapped when he started screaming. "I'm not dying. I told your ass to knock on the door, and you didn't, so now you have to deal with this." That bathroom break-in was quickly followed by an impromptu "birds and bees" conversation that I was not ready to give and he wasn't ready to receive, but that had to go down anyway because he'd forced my hand.

The biggest test of all, though, was helping my son work through the anger that came from not having his father around. I never told Mark he couldn't be in his son's life; in fact, I welcomed and encouraged his presence. But when we broke up and went our separate ways, Mark first had to work on getting himself on a stronger emotional footing. My father played an important role in that; after the big fight that ended with Mark hitting me, my dad took my son's father under his wing and schooled him on the value of controlling his emotions. He did that because he wanted Mark to be in his son's life, and he knew that the only way that could happen was if my ex grew himself up a bit and learned how to express himself without the anger. In Mark, my father saw himself, and he deep-dived into helping Mark navigate around the same destructive land mines that nearly destroyed my father and could have easily obliterated his relationship with me. "You can't spend your whole life walking around mad at the world," my father recalled telling Mark repeatedly. "You have to be a positive example for your son, so he can be better than both of us. That's what a good father wants for his child."

Eventually, Mark got more involved in our son's life. I'd moved to Los Angeles to pursue my career, but I would send Marcell to my father's house for the summers so that they could have that father-son bond Marcell craved but couldn't get while in California with me. Dad would have Marcell out in the backyard of his house in the suburbs, hunting frogs, making art projects in his metal workshop, play-fighting with makeshift swords they built with wrapping-paper rolls. Mark would join in on the fun, or he'd take Marcell for the afternoon to visit with his mom or his other children. At some point, Mark thought he'd gotten himself together enough to actually ask if our son could move back to DC to live with him and his girlfriend. It was a novel idea; a boy needs his daddy. I know this deep down in my soul. But I didn't trust that Mark was ready to care for Marcell full-time. He was living with a woman I didn't know, and his living and employment situation were still sketchy as far as I was concerned. "I'm not comfortable with that," I said as gently as I could. "I mean, you don't even have a landline. How am I supposed to send my son three thousand miles away from me and you don't even have a landline? I'm just not comfortable with that."

"Taraji, come on," he insisted. "My mom is here, she can help out—"

"But Marcell is not her responsibility," I interrupted. "He is my responsibility and yours." Mark was upset, but he recognized that there was truth in what I was saying. Finally, he let it go.

. . .

Marcell and I went home to DC in 2002 for the holidays. We had our annual Christmas dinner at his mother's house; all of his children were there, as were their mothers, and my friend Pam and her husband, Mark's best friend. From the moment I walked in the door, something felt off. I couldn't put my finger on what it was, but when Mark's eyes met mine, I had a weird, dark feeling—call it a mother's intuition. I was heartened, though, to see him interact with Marcell—to see the two of them connecting in the way only fathers and sons can. I even witnessed Mark parent Marcell as the two played tic-tac-toe at the dining room table.

The game wasn't going well; Marcell was yelling, upset that he'd lost several rounds in a row to his father. Mark put his hand on his shoulder and schooled him: "Let me tell you something, son," he told Marcell. "Don't you let anger control your life the way it did mine. Use your head, black man."

What he was saying was practically word for word what my father had told Mark over the years as he struggled with his own anger. I'll never forget the sound of Mark's words or the look in his eyes as he talked to our son. Love was there.

That would be the last Christmas Marcell would see his father.

We left for Los Angeles right after the New Year, with Marcell settling back into school and me into work, our hearts full from the quality time we'd spent with our family. But only three weeks later, on January 25, 2003, I got an early-morning phone call from Mark's mother that woke me out of my sleep. The second I heard her voice—the way she said my name and how her words shook in her throat—I knew Mark was gone.

"Mark was killed last night," she said.

My heart stopped beating.

My first love, the father of my precious son, was gone from here—taken at the tender age of thirty-three. I wasn't ready for him to go. None of us were. He had so much more living to do, so much more loving. But God had other plans. As I lay in my bed, crying and praying for Mark's soul, my mind kept wandering back to the dream sequence in the movie *Baby Boy*. In the scene, Yvette, crying, bruised, and in the throes of sexual passion with Jody just moments after he punches her in the eye, imagines herself laughing with her son's father, visiting him in prison, and then, dressed in black, standing hand in hand with her son as the two of them gaze at her first love's body lying dead in a coffin. The connection was so powerful, particularly that scene; when we'd filmed it some three years earlier, I'd been hyperemotional, as the entire movie in general and the fight and dream sequence scenes in particular were unfolding in front of the cameras just as I was still processing my own personal drama with Mark and our volatile relationship. Watch the scene closely and you'll see the physical manifestation of my anxiety; I'd lost at least ten pounds during the filming, mostly from the stress of acting out what I'd just lived through. My clothes look like they're resting on a hanger, I'm so thin.

The first non–family member I called after Mark's mom told me he'd died was John Singleton. "The dream came true," I said, sobbing.

"What do you mean?" John asked.

"My son's father was killed and I have to go to the funeral with my son."

. . .

Marcell was nine when I took him by the hand, walked him to his father's casket, and helped him say his final farewell. He was too young to understand the full implications of what was going on; all he knew was that he would never see his father again, and his mother was extremely upset. As I sat in the pew sobbing, Marcell, ever the comforter, ever my protector, rubbed my back, doing his best to soothe me. I wiped my tears as I listened to the choir sing Mark home, then turned toward Marcell to give him a reassuring look that I hoped would say, "Mommy is okay, and I appreciate you looking after me." But when I looked in my son's direction, something in his hand caught my attention: it was a beige rubber band, the same color, shape, and length of the rubber bands Mark, an office clerk, loved to play with. He used to fashion them into huge rubber band balls, and kept them all around him—at work, at his apartment, in the car.

"Where did you get that rubber band?" I whispered to Marcell as he pulled on it and slung it between his fingers.

"I found it on the floor right there," he whispered back, pointing at the floor beneath the pew in front of us.

When I took Marcell up to the coffin to see his father for the last time, he had that rubber band in his hand. "Do you want to put it in there with your dad?" I asked my son as he peered into the casket.

"Yes," Marcell said quietly.

He tucked that rubber band into his father's hand, and we slowly returned back to our seats.

• • •

I'll always miss Mark, my one true love, but his absence was much more acute for my son, particularly after my father died, leaving him without a male figure in his life, burning out his joy just as he matured and the fire of adolescence and hormones built up. By the time he started high school in 2008, he was shutting down—refusing to talk, angry, depressed, smoking a lot of weed. I'm a fairly liberal parent; I believe most things are okay in moderation. But I knew my son, who was using marijuana to numb his pain of not having a father around, was overdoing it. He was missing the guidance he craved as he was becoming a man, though my father pitched in as much as could from afar. There are no two ways about it: boys need their fathers. No matter how hard I tried, no matter how much I depended on his basketball coaches to step in and instruct him on how to tie a tie or how to dress for specific occasions or how to comport himself as a sportsman and gentleman on and off the court, no matter how much he picked up from his friends who had dads in their homes, Marcell needed more: he needed his father to show him how to walk this earth as a black man.

The impact of not having a father around came to a head in high school, when, finally, the questions, along with the anger, started flying. By then, he was asking outright: "Where was my dad? Where was he?" It was a question that had been bubbling in his heart from as early as the eighth grade, but that I didn't realize until we found ourselves in joint therapy sessions, trying to figure out the source of my son's anger and depression. When the therapist helped us finally put our finger on it, I went back to old photos of my son to see when, exactly, his face began to betray those feelings he said he'd held on to for so long. Sure enough, it was there; I had missed it. There were all these pictures of him in elementary school and seventh grade, with this goofy grin and bright eyes, looking happy. And then in one picture of him in the eighth grade, there was barely a smirk, and the light in his eyes had dimmed. Where there had been joy, there was nothing. I was devastated, and beat myself up for a long time after that for not noticing then that my baby needed therapy—a place where we could dig out all of the emotional muck that came from Marcell's holding in his feelings about his father's absence.

I, too, am culpable for my son's emotional fragility—I know that. It was while I was away filming my role as Joss Carter on the

CBS show *Person of Interest* that his anger came to a head. I agreed to a two-year commitment to film in New York out of love for my son and parental duty: I needed the money to take care of my kid. High school was $30,000 per year, and then there were uniforms and books, extracurricular fees, and the like, on top of the expense of feeding, clothing, and housing him. Plus, I was thinking about college tuition—being able to knock out the cost of at least four years without having to worry about the bill. I asked his permission and he was gung-ho for my opportunity. Marcell said he understood why I was leaving. I was resting easy when I left because my mother agreed to leave her home in Maryland and move to California to be with my son while I worked—a huge blessing considering she left all she knew, her family, friends, and way of life, to hold my life together. While there, I parented the best way I knew how: I Skyped with my son regularly, kept in touch with his teachers and coaches, checked in with my mom to make sure the two of them had everything they needed, and flew back to California whenever I could so that we could spend quality time together, no matter if I had as little as two days to spare.

Still, my son needed me to be physically present. He wasn't happy. I wasn't happy. My mama wasn't happy. It was the hardest time of our lives. The little boy in Marcell needed his mother more than I knew, precisely because I wasn't there to help him unpack and work through the emotions that came from being fatherless. Even though I gave him the world—the life I could only dream of as a kid—he wasn't fulfilled. There was no way he could wrap his mind around the loss of his father and grandfather. Money couldn't buy that for him.

In therapy, we had to walk through fire and it was painful.

Accusations of my not being home with him full-time flew, and I was neither prepared nor willing to swallow that pill. "I didn't have a choice!" I yelled. "This is what it is. These kids you're hanging around with, their moms don't work and they're eating Snickers and Cheetos for breakfast, but you want to tell me what I'm not doing? I'm bringing home the bacon, cooking it despite working all these crazy hours, and making sure your ass is eating something besides Snickers and Cheetos. When I did have to be away from you, I made sure the next-best substitute was there: my mother. Don't talk to me about what I didn't do." I threw in a few expletives so he knew how very serious I was.

In another session, I had to come clean to him on why his father and I broke up. That was a tough one. Until then, I'd kept to myself the details of his dad verbally abusing and hitting me because I didn't want to sully Marcell's image of him, but in therapy, it was clear he needed to know why we broke up so that he could begin the long road toward closure. The pain in his eyes and his rage in response to the revelation hurt me to my core. "But why would you hit my mother!" he yelled, punching the pillows decorating the therapist's couch where we sat.

"Marcell, baby, you have to let this go," I reasoned, physically holding on to my son to restrain and try to calm him down. "You can't carry this hate in your heart. I'm sure that if your father had to do it all again, he wouldn't have hit me, but he learned from it and I did, too. And you know not to ever do it, either."

It was hard work, but therapy did wonders to help him—to help us—get healthy and back on the good foot. Of course, it didn't solve all of our problems, and, like adolescents everywhere, my son acted out in ways that got him into hot water with me.

Like the time he scratched up my brand-new Porsche—not even a month old and barely driven—taking it out of the garage for a joyride. He never even made it out of the driveway, he was so scared of what he'd done. He tried to cover up the scratch with a black Sharpie, but he ultimately came clean to me. Then there was the time Marcell got caught sneaking out. He was seventeen and still fighting maturity. I recognize that he was old enough to be separate from and independent of his mom, but in my house, I had rules. If I told my son he couldn't go out, well, he better get comfortable on the sofa, pick up a book or find a show to watch on the television, because he wasn't going to going out—simple as that. As much as it had irked me as a child, I'd adopted my mother's no-nonsense, "do exactly as I say, or else" style of parenting that I'd made a point of obeying when I was younger.

Marcell wasn't on the same page this one particular night. I'd come home from an event, gone only about three hours, only to find my son knocked out in his room and the entire house smelling like weed. I yanked his ass off the bed. "I thought we had a promise!" I yelled. "I thought you weren't smoking anymore!"

"I'm not," he said, groggily.

I'd already spotted a bag of weed sitting on his sink counter—meaning that not only was he breaking that promise, but also lying to my face. I snatched the bag and waved it in front of him. "Well what is this?" I demanded.

At my wits' end, I did only what, in that moment, I could think to do. "You don't want to act right? Get out." I handed him his cell phone. "Call whoever's house and tell them to come get you."

Marcell dialed someone's number, but whoever it was didn't

pick up. He left at least two messages before I demanded he hand his phone over. "Where your friends now? Oh, nobody's picking up? You see who your only ally is?"

We argued some more until he got so angry he reared up at me like he was going to strike. "You don't want to do that, son. See, you not hood. You not 'bout that life. Hit me. Please hit me so I can have a reason to take your ass out!" Tears streaming down his face, Marcell stood right there and took that, because he knew hitting me would be the death of him. Ghetto Betty—my alter ego—is unpredictable, and neither of us can promise you what's going to happen when she comes all the way out. "Now where's that ride?"

"It'll be here!"

"Oh, it's coming? Fine. Get your ass out." And with that, I pushed Marcell out the door and locked it.

There we were, the two of us on either side of the door, a world away from one another as we both struggled our way through this new phase in our relationship. He was on the cusp of manhood, trying to get his shit together, and I was in the throes of mothering an adult, understanding it was time to loosen the reins but unable to let go of my hold. He was outside—quiet, seething. I was inside, quiet, seething. Soon enough, taillights were shining in my window, and my son was gone. I had his phone, thus no way of contacting him, and because it was locked, I couldn't call any of his friends to check up on him and make sure he was okay. I sat up all night, racked with worry.

The next day, Marcell came home, head hung low—broken. He had no idea I had it in me to put him out, but he understood it when I broke it down to him. "You're not going to be here driving me crazy," I said calmly as we sat at the dining room table, trying to work out our issues. "I'm not going to die of worry over you when I know I've done my job. You have no other choice but to get it together or die trying. I really do not know what else to tell you besides that."

. . .

Raising Marcell has been a journey, one that I loved him through. With prayer, therapy, candid talk, and love, he came through on the other side. My son is smiling again. The life is back in his eyes. He's an aspiring rapper, producer, and music engineer, with a keen sense of self, and he pours into his music all the memories, passion, and sentiment he has about his experiences growing up as a black male without a father, and the dynamics of being one of only a handful of black boys in an all-white school. This is pain and isolation that many people know—no matter their color, background, or economic status—and rather than stew in it, Marcell is using all that creativity running through his DNA to lift his voice and let people who can identify with his struggle know that they're not alone and that this, too, shall pass.

He's wearing his maturity and growth on his sleeve now. I took Marcell with me to Monte Carlo recently, and while I was working at an appearance with the producers and cast of *Empire,* my son gravitated toward the men and started kicking it with the show's creator, Danny Strong, Terrence Howard, and Webb, a man on Terrence's security team. Next thing I knew, they were huddling together, having "man talk." When they were finished, Terrence, Danny, and Webb gave me the rundown. "Man," Danny said. "You did a good job. He's got his head on right."

That came from me fighting for my child. That was the advice I got from Mark, my makeup artist on the set of *The Division*. I sat in his chair one morning with the weight of the world on my shoulders, crying so hard over Marcell that Mark had to stop applying my foundation until I pulled it together. He put his hand on my shoulder and looked at my reflection in the mirror. What he said to me, I'll never forget: "Don't ever give up on him."

There were times when I wanted to, believe me. If I had a dollar for every time I called my friend Pam and her husband, Jerry, to tell them I was packing Marcell's clothes and sending him their way, I could have retired a decade ago. But I hung in there, and so did my son. And now he gets it. The cards he writes on special occasions confirm what I know to be true. "Mom, you loved me when I didn't want to love myself."

It's something when your child finally understands.

9

Breathing Life into Art

Paradoxically, miraculously, it was Daddy's death that helped teach me about the power of art. Daddy got saved after my grandmother died—walked up to the baptismal pool dressed in that crisp early-Sunday-morning white, held out both his strong, battered hands in submission, folded them over his heart, and, in the arms of the pastor, went under that water and then came back up new. After that, trouble didn't last. There was no more drinking and fighting and tearing up the good that moved in his life. He focused, instead, on delivering on the promises he boasted for anyone who had ears: he got himself a good woman, a house with a garage to do his metalwork, a pickup truck, and a Harley, too. He wanted to be a better man. His mother, who had been hard on him, was gone from here, and he needed to give her in death what he'd had a hard time giving her when she walked this earth: the very best of him.

As it happened, we got to see the married, Bible-thumping,

polished Boris Lawrence Henson only for a little while. My father was incredibly intuitive, and he knew deep down in his gut that he was going to die the same way his mother did, and he was just about right: pancreatic cancer stole her breath; liver cancer put my father in the ground fourteen years later. In my dad's case, cirrhosis of the liver, the result of years of drinking, made his organ so hard it was rendered inoperable, leaving the cancer to fester and grow and have its way with my father's body.

Somehow, though, we expected Daddy to make it; he was our warrior and often reminded us of his strength. "Get your scrawny ass out of here," he'd snap, curling his biceps into mounds of muscle. "I'm Mandingo! Big Daddy!" But from the cancer, no amount of muscle could save him. He grew weaker and wearier by the day, and all I could do was watch.

It was a rainy, bitterly cold February night in 2006 when my father started taking that slow, torturous walk toward his final day. My stepmother crumpled her body on the bed alongside my father, the only thing keeping her from falling to the floor in overwhelming grief. She'd just witnessed my father throw up what looked like coffee grounds—curdles of blood that had accumulated in his body as his organs began shutting down. I caught a glimpse of the doctor shaking his head. "What does that mean?" I asked him.

The doctor swallowed his words. "He's bleeding internally," he said finally, his face grim.

"Talk to me!" I demanded. "Is this it for him?"

"Basically," the doctor said simply. He gently touched my shoulder, no doubt to console me. But his fingers felt heavy, like bricks.

I turned back toward my father's room, struggling through a pool of tears to get a glimpse of my dying father—my hero. My stepmother was still lying on him. "I'm not ready for him to go," she said, crying. "I'm not ready."

My father was awake. Though he couldn't talk, I could tell from the tenderness in his touch that he was making calculations. He wasn't going to die with my stepmother in the room. He couldn't do that to her. He would fight. And when he let go, it would be with me by his side because he trusted me to let him walk out of the land of the living.

Another day passed before the rain broke and the sun emerged through the clouds; I got up and snatched open the curtains. It was a perfect day. I knew it would be my worst day, too. *Dad is going home today,* I said to myself, sighing, resigned but scared.

I went to the hospital to relieve my stepmother, who'd been with my dad all night. Always, there was someone there with him. I hung around that hospital the entire day, watching, listening. Praying. Daddy grew weaker and weaker throughout the day, going in and out of consciousness as I rubbed his hands, adjusted his sheets, and tried to get him to take his pills and sips of water. Finally, Daddy made his final rally: he bolted up in his bed. I looked in his eyes, so much like mine: piercing, dark, doelike. He stared back at me, a novel's worth of love story flashing across his face, even though he couldn't say a word. I didn't know what to say or if I should say anything at all, whether to tell him one more time that I loved him, or if I should simply relish that quiet moment between father and child. I chose the latter. "Lean on my back, Dad," I said, helping him fall onto my body. Together, we sat there, resting on each other. Quiet.

That would be our last moment together. Not long after he laid back down, my father, wild-eyed, started clawing at all the tubes and wires sticking out of his body. I'd read somewhere that just before some humans die, they start scratching at their skin—like their soul is trying to get out—and this is exactly what my father was doing. Trying to get free. My lips quivered as I leaned down to my father's ear. "Dad, if you're ready to go, let go," I whispered. "We're going to be all right."

Daddy stopped scratching and pulling and shifted his eyes over to me. Then, after a beat, his entire body started jerking as he threw up a fresh round of coffee grounds. Blood was everywhere.

I bolted out of the room and out into the hallway, the fluorescent lights practically blinding me as I ran, crying and screaming. The beeping of the machines in my father's room rang like sirens, echoing down the halls. "Code blue!" I heard someone yell.

It was such a violent way to die.

My father was fifty-eight. He was there with me when I took my first breath, and I was there when he took his last.

So furious was the loss, so immense, that the only way I thought possible to deal, to breathe, to put one foot in front of the other after he passed, was to bury my feelings about his death six feet down in my gut, where no one could access it. I had to compartmentalize his death and my emotions because there was work to be done: just three days after my father passed, I had to sing "It's Hard Out Here for a Pimp," a hit song from *Hustle & Flow*, at the 78th Academy Awards, which had nominated it for Best Original Song, a first in the category for a hip hop song. "I'm fine," I would say when family and friends asked me how I was faring. "He's in a better place," and "He's with God," and

"He's not hurting anymore" were my go-to responses—the easiest way to get those who knew and loved me to think that, really, I was okay. Sometimes, saying those things out loud made me believe them, too. They kept my emotions in check. I needed to make peace with it and quickly, or I would break. I was the child of Mandingo Warrior. Breaking wasn't an option. At least, that's what I told myself.

But my heart wouldn't cooperate. It was shattered. Unbeknownst to my family and friends, I'd slipped into a deep depression, rendering me incapable of dealing with my father's death, particularly after witnessing him pass away. Through my tears, all I could visualize was his face and the moments when he was throwing up blood. I was desperate to know if he knew how much I loved him and whether I should have told him just one more time. I was in so much pain: it seared every part of my being and I couldn't figure out how to deal with the agony.

But God has a way of using our work to help us process our pain. Soon after my father's death, I started production as a principal actress in the critically acclaimed feature film *The Curious Case of Benjamin Button* opposite Brad Pitt and Cate Blanchett. In the movie, set in New Orleans in 1918, I play Queenie, the lead caregiver in a nursing home. It is there that Queenie wipes behinds and fixes supper and corrals old women who "lose" strings of pearls they're too senile to know are resting pretty on their necks, and where, too, she deals with death all day. She also makes room in her heart for a mysterious baby left on the nursing home's stoop—an infant, born old and ugly and oddly afflicted and white. After the initial shock, the single, barren, God-fearing black woman loves that baby with the entirety of her huge heart and blinks not once at the fact that as he grows up, Benjamin is aging in reverse. Queenie, then, becomes the very embodiment of acceptance; the way she parents her adopted son gives him—and the film itself—the emotional anchor necessary for Benjamin to fully inhabit his place in the world and also to accept unequivocally those who come into his life broken, hurting, different.

The irony of my playing that role at that specific time, after I'd just finished holding my dad's hand as he walked through death's door, was rich. Queenie was a sort of death doula in her own right—a woman charged with helping the elderly make that long, slow, final transition. Playing her forced me to deal with death every day. I couldn't run from it. Not as Queenie and not as Taraji.

What's more, the way Queenie raised Benjamin mirrored the way Boris Henson parented his own child. During the most tumultuous parts of his life, my dad was a lot of things—an alcoholic, economically unstable, a domestic abuser—and he did a lot of things wrong. Still, time and again, he would show me that no matter how often you fall from grace, what matters most is how many times you get up. Through example, he showed me that we're human—that nobody is perfect and there most certainly isn't a rulebook for living a perfect life. Though my dad was no longer around to lead me to this thinking, the lessons he had interlaced throughout my childhood and adolescent years, the times we bonded over simple things like go-go music or blue crabs, seeped like water into the cracks of Queenie's heart, into the reservoir of love and regard she had for Benjamin's humanity. As hard as I tried to hide my immense sadness over his death, as diligent as I thought I was about compartmentalizing my emotions and walling off my heart so that I could deep-dive into the work, I couldn't keep Daddy away. He was right there with me. Always there.

That's how powerful art is. It can turn hearts of stone into pulsing mounds of mush. It can turn a raving racist into an empathetic person with the capacity to reach across divides. It can help a grieving daughter lean into a tremendous loss and, in the process, create magic.

Art uncovers the truth. My driving force is that truth; it is my full intention to breathe it into each of my characters, no matter how pretty or ugly they are, whether I agree with them or not. Maybe God put an extra dose of truth serum in my blood, but when the director yells "action" and the camera is on, I can't lie. I have no mask. The truth manifests itself on my face—in every word I say, in every movement I make. I inhabit my character and my character me, from the top of my head to the tips of my pedicured toes. There have been times when the synergy between the two is so powerful—the energy of real life and the darkness and pain I'm channeling for the camera—that the characters creep into my dreams. It is spiritual, trance-inducing, even, if I let it move through my body honestly.

I learned how to do this in theater, where we actors don't have the safety of second and third takes and a director yelling, "Cut—let's try that again, except this time, do it this way." Onstage, the audience is a living being that draws breath from our words, our movement, our inflections; it is up to us actors to reach deep inside ourselves to make every eye in the house tear up, to make every stomach push up a belly-twisting laugh, to make every heart really feel your deepest pain and your most sensual touch. In other words, we performers have to be fully available to all of our emotions—to deal with our shit in real life. If we're missing it in real life, we're missing it on the playwright's or screenwriter's page. There was no way I could bury my father in the recesses of my heart when I was charged with being a parent on camera.

Harnessing that emotion requires a willingness not only to open up, but also to pay attention. I love to study human behavior; I get off on riding my bike through the park and taking note of how a young mother sighs when she leans down into her stroller and catches a glimpse of her baby's tiny, puckering lips, or the grimace in the face of a jogger pushing through the last step of his run. It's not a thing, either, for me to linger over dinner at a restaurant just to survey the way a woman's eyes flicker in the candlelight when her date looks into them for the first time. I even study myself; one time I got so angry my fury manifested itself in my hands. I literally stopped yelling and said to myself, *Damn, do you see how your fingers tremble when you're mad?* Harnessing the emotions and taking note of human behavior is what strips away the agendas and exposes the art. It releases both me and the characters I play.

Take, for instance, Shug, the pregnant, thumb-sucking prostitute I portrayed in *Hustle & Flow*. The first time I read the screenplay, I closed the last page, plopped the script on my nightstand, and shook my head. How in the world would I convince moviegoers to be sympathetic to the plight of a ho? I'm not prostitute material; there's no way I'd ever let a pimp control my mind. I had to figure out how to hide my power and let Shug shine, but in an unexpected way. Playing her as a dumb, slow ho that nobody cared about would have been much too easy and obvious. And, as I found as I got to know my character, it would have been dishonest, too.

If I wanted Shug to defy caricature and stereotype, she and I would have to become more than acquaintances; we needed to be one. So, as I do with all my characters, I deep-dived into the script, swimming beyond the page, learning not just the words that would be coming out of Shug's mouth, but every thought, experience, attitude, and inflection that informed them. I'd take her with me in the car and ask her, "Whose baby is that in your belly?" and then when I pulled into the driveway, I'd say, "Do you even like kids?" I'd pace the kitchen with yogurt in one hand and the script in the other, and I'd say out loud, "You ever consider stabbing that muthafucka DJay, the pimp, in his sleep?" Some days, I'd scream out when Shug talked back to me. "I'm not stupid," she told me one night while I lounged in my living room. "I'm scared and in love!" I screamed so loud my dog, Uncle Willie, jumped and started barking like he'd seen a stranger running through the house. In a sense, he *was* seeing someone unfamiliar. Shug was there.

When we got closer to principal production, I spent some time in Shug's world, down in the modest shotgun houses of Memphis, Tennessee, where it was sticky and bleak and hotter than the Fourth of July. Between table reads, run-throughs, and costume fittings, Terrence Howard, who played DJay, a pimp struggling to become a rapper, Anthony Anderson, who portrayed an underappreciated hip hop producer hopeful, and a few of the other cast members and I ran all through the hood, riding through its dustiest back streets and posting up in the cramped, sweltering living rooms of its residents, trying to find a little respite from the sun as we got to know the people for real. It was there that I found Shug's rhythm, where I felt her weight. It was different from that of single black girls in DC—different from that of poor, desperate women in Chicago and Detroit. This Memphis weight was distinct—country and dusty and slow and thick, like that which I'd never before lifted.

· · ·

Tucked into one of those living rooms was a girl who immediately made me think of Shug. Not that she was anything like Shug, necessarily. There was just something about her. She had on pum pum shorts and a tank top highlighting her cleavage and a weave framing her baby face. A tattoo crept up her right thigh; I think it was Snoopy. When she turned her head toward the light, the sun glinted against her gold tooth.

"I'm Kissy," she said, giggling.

"What you say? Keishi?" I asked, struggling to pick up her accent.

"No. It's Kissy," she said, interrupting her answer to make kissing noises, "like kissy."

We talked and laughed and talked and laughed some more, each of us letting down our guards as the moments turned to minutes and the minutes stretched to hours. They mimicked my DC accent, I mimicked their deep southern drawl; they'd laugh at me and I'd laugh at them. Kissy stood out to me because she had this sweetness about her. Plus, something about Memphis reminded me of the summers I spent with my grandmother in North Carolina when I was a child: I'd gone to the mall and seen a few girls with chests full of baby powder to keep themselves cool, just like my grandmother used to rub on her chest and mine, too, when the thermometer crept so high the only reasonable thing to do was to sweat.

Kissy became the heart of my Shug.

She was nowhere on the screenwriter's 120-page script; there, Shug was just a skeleton. It was my job as a trained actress to give her skin and fat and blood and DNA—to put the twang in her tongue and the fear deep in her bones and the hope in her heart. But I couldn't build her until I opened my eyes to see *all* of her.

My job is to make sure that everyone else *sees* my characters, too. On the first day of filming, I showed up to the set with a prosthetic on my belly, a bare face, and a bad weave, plus a gold tooth. "She's gotta have a gold tooth," I'd insisted earlier, stating my case to the director, Craig Brewer, and to the head of wardrobe. "Terrence has one, so guess what: If Shug's a bottom bitch, who she looking up to?" Craig stared at me, waiting for the answer. "Him. Her man. Why she ain't got a gold tooth? She needs one just like DJay's."

I was feeling good about Shug when I showed up to film the first scene. I had to open the front door to the messy, sweltering house she shared with two other prostitutes, a baby, and her pimp, and there was filth on top of filth and bodies on top of bodies and Shug was pregnant and hot and sweaty. Shit was about to get real. But just before Craig yelled action, I yelled, "Hold up!" I'd seen a bottle of baby powder out of the corner of my eye; I grabbed it, peeled my dress from my skin, and dumped a few puffs of the sweet-smelling dust down the front of my breasts and neck. I smacked my hands together to get rid of the excess powder and tossed the bottle back to the spot where the props guy had originally placed it.

"Okay, go!" I said, taking my place by the door.

Craig yelled, "Cut!" and burst out laughing. "You're fucking brilliant!" he hollered.

That moment happened because Taraji was no longer in the room; Shug was. She was neither dumb nor slow; she had a backstory that mattered. She'd been abused, making her easy prey, even for a sorry pimp like DJay, but she had a bit of fight to her, like, if she got that chance, if somebody sowed a good seed in her, she would be an incredible citizen. I hid my power so that the audience could see Shug's quiet strength anchor her ragtag family, even and especially when it seemed it was all falling to pieces.

I think this is what distinguishes me—what makes me a different kind of actress. I have the gift of being able to see what sometimes neither the creator nor the director can see. This is what an actor is supposed to do; we are not robots, but humans who, if we're worth our salt, see beyond the page and deep into our character's soul. I gravitate toward characters like Shug, Yvette, Cookie, and Queenie to give them some kind of royalty they wouldn't necessarily see in their own circumstances—to illuminate them and tell their story so that the audience knows what I know. They matter.

Sometimes my characters pay me in kind.

On the same day that we filmed the death of Queenie in *Benjamin Button,* my cousin Daniel passed away. Understand this: losing him was like losing a rib, particularly coming as it did on the heels of my father's death. Compounding the loss was that the day of my cousin's January 2007 funeral was the day we shot

Queenie's funeral for the film, and naturally I was upset because I couldn't say my final good-byes to the man I'd loved and respected. My patience was thin, and the littlest things were agitating me, particularly the prosthetics that were placed on my hands to make them look as old as Queenie was. For some reason, the prosthetic on my left hand kept lifting.

"You better come fix this!" I warned the makeup team. David Fincher, the director of *Benjamin Button,* was very meticulous, and if he saw even a hint of that hand being out of order, there would be problems. Still, no matter how much they fussed over that hand, it wouldn't get right.

David had barely called it a night when I rushed to the phone to call my godmother to ask her about the funeral. "How did everything go?" I asked.

"It was beautiful," she said, "except rigor mortis started setting in, in his left hand. They couldn't get his hand to lie right in the casket."

What a gift to know that Queenie allowed me and my cousin to be together one last time. Acting is communication, not only person to person, but soul to soul—a physical, emotional, and certainly spiritual expression. When I get it right, it is life itself.

10
Building Characters

When Richard Pryor was at the height of his powers, I was only a kid, so there was no way for me to understand the rhythm of his work as a humorist, writer, actor, and producer, or the nuances that danced in his jokes, which oozed attitude, and were unapologetic in their demand to look, *really look,* at the absurdities of our deeply complex lives. On his stage, no secret was safe. Societal wounds, formed by the shrapnel of race, poverty, misogyny, and insecurity, were ripped open and poked at under his harsh, unrelenting spotlight, and the characters he portrayed onstage—junkies, monsters, old southern gentlemen, hustlers, lovers, even Richard Pryor himself—screamed out in agony but told their tales anyway, always with a biting humor that made the audience laugh and think and feel. Pryor was an incredible entertainer and arguably the world's greatest comedian, but he was, above all else, a stellar storyteller who believed in exposing the truth.

I wasn't ready for Richard Pryor's truth the first time I saw him on the big screen. My father took me to his 1982 concert movie, *Richard Pryor: Live on the Sunset Strip*, the first big comeback stand-up routine he'd done after nearly burning himself alive in a drug-and-alcohol mishap two years earlier. I was twelve.

To be fair to my father, I did beg him to let me see it. I was raised on a steady diet of comedy—my adoration for the on-screen shenanigans of Carol Burnett, Lucille Ball, Goldie Hawn, and the like knew no bounds—and Richard Pryor, a significant stroke in the pop-cultural landscape of my childhood, was a part of that pantheon of comedians that I respected, even if my mom wouldn't let me see most of his films. Mommy took those R ratings seriously, so she wasn't about to buy her preadolescent daughter movie tickets to see Pryor flicks like *Bustin' Loose, Stir Crazy, Greased Lightning,* and *Which Way Is Up?*. Instead I had to live on what I read about him in magazines like *Ebony* and *Jet,* and rely on the Richard Pryor jokes I heard secondhand while eavesdropping around family dinners and backyard barbecues on grown-up conversation, which always seemed to eventually veer into what the comedian had done, said, or joked about in his movies and stand-up routine recordings. But *Live on the Sunset Strip* was one that, by hook or by crook, I was going to see—with or without my mother's permission. I knew my father would not say no to me.

"Now listen here, he gonna be saying some things," my father warned. "You ain't ready for that shit."

"But Daddy, please!" I begged. "I love him! He's so funny."

My father narrowed his eyes and looked at me sideways, like this was going to determine whether I could handle all that came with a Richard Pryor joint. I clasped my hands together in the classic begging position, smiled my smile, blinked my eyes, and bounced around excitedly while he silently pondered the implications of taking a twelve-year-old to hear some Pryor stand-up. "Please, Daddy, please!" I said, bouncing around.

"You're gonna be uncomfortable," my dad said. "He's talking about sex and shit."

"I don't care," I insisted. "I want to see it."

Finally, Dad caved. "Okay. Don't tell your mother I took you."

A few days later, well after it was dark, way after the average twelve-year-old would have bathed, climbed into her pajamas, and said her evening prayers, Daddy and I piled onto a Washington, DC, bus headed all the way up Sixteenth Street, into a nice white neighborhood teeming with expensive restaurants, bars, and lots of revelers, drunk, cursing, and hopping from club to club looking for their next bit of fun. Dad and I arrived just in time for the ten o' clock show; after he got me settled in my seat, my father took a beer out of his jacket pocket, drank it, then promptly fell asleep, leaving me to decipher all on my own Richard Pryor's commentary on prison, the mafia, masturbation, orgasms, Africa, the word "nigger," and freebasing. I mean, Richard Pryor said some things, and for the most part, I laughed, but God, I was uncomfortable and embarrassed and ready to melt into that seat. Finally, just as the credits began to roll, Daddy woke up and stretched like it was a new day, then looked over at me and saw my face, wide-eyed and contorted in a combination of horror, fascination, and wonder. Dad laughed his ass off.

"I told yo ass!" he said when he finally composed himself. "Now come on. And don't tell your mother."

I kept my mouth shut. But I never, ever forgot the experience, and later, when I had the opportunity to really dig deep into Richard Pryor's films and stand-up routines, I came to appreciate the intricacy of his humor—how each of his characters, whether wrapped in a joke or prancing across the big screen, revealed something deeper than what was on the surface. A nine-year-old masturbating in a tub wasn't so much a nasty little boy as he was a kid on a journey to discovering his body; an aggrieved husband shooting up his own car to spite his wife is angry, but he's also proud that the car is proof he's a good provider; a backwater country man who runs into Dracula may be too ignorant to know he's facing off against a killer, but he's observant, confident, and skilled enough to pick at the vampire's flaws and fend him off with insulting, cutting words. Each of those revelations, and so many more, goes to the heart of his characters' humanity, revealing what ultimately rules their actions: insecurity, fear, racism, boredom, empathy, lust, wonder.

This, to me, made Richard Pryor not only funny, but also a master teacher—one of the first entertainers to reveal to me the importance of going deeper than what is on the page. He used his body. He made noises and faces. His sighs and well-timed chuckles and the way he could shrink himself, this superstar, bigger than life, into a pile of everyman vulnerability, made me connect with him. I got the same from watching Lucille Ball and Carol Burnett, Goldie Hawn, Bette Davis, and Tom Hanks, too, each of them masters at transforming themselves—masters at creating iconic characters.

I live for iconic characters. Think Angela Bassett in *Waiting to Exhale,* when she runs through the closet of her soon-to-be ex-husband, rambling on and on about being the sucker for putting her man above herself, only to have him stomp her heart into the ground. Who can forget the sight of her ripping his expensive suits off the hangers, piling them all into his fancy car, striking that match, lighting her cigarette, tossing the tiny flame on top of that beautiful ride then stomping down the driveway, the inferno behind her matching the rage in her eyes? We'll never stop talking, either, about Angela's star turn in *What's Love Got to Do with It,* a transformation into the superstar Tina Turner so thorough in its innocence, weariness, fear, and drive that it doesn't occur to us viewers until the end of the film, when it transitions into a real-life Tina Turner stage performance, that Angela is only *playing* Tina, and is not the actual singer herself.

This is what I love, too, about Sanaa Lathan, an incredible actress whose performance in the 2000 rom com *Love & Basketball* was downright transformative. She literally disappeared into her character, Monica, an ambitious but frustrated college basketball player desperate in her pursuit of both stardom on the court and love with a childhood friend who is as passionate about the sport as she. I know Sanaa. She is as far from a tomboy as they come—all curves and soft, pink, and girly. But on-screen, she was a cornrow-wearing, six-pack-having baller with a sportsman's heart and a disgust for makeup and tight dresses. There's one scene in particular that stands out to me as the finest example yet of her ability to turn herself inside out and become Monica, so much so that Sanaa disappears. In it, she's playing an intense high school game in front of a coach scouting Monica for the roster of a college team she's desperate to play for, when she misses a potentially game-winning shot and has to foul out in order to give her team the chance to win without her. Forced to deal with the disappointment and embarrassment of failing her team, Monica stalks over to the sidelines and literally hides from the crowd, fighting back her tears while she buries her face in the folds of her jersey. What was incredible to me as an actress was Sanaa's choice to make the scene not about the tears, but the hiding. I watch a mind-numbing number of movies—for work, for pleasure, to study, to learn—and today I remember that scene, more than fifteen years old, as though I watched it five minutes ago. That's acting. That's iconic.

. . .

I think the transformation is rooted in actors' commitment to their characters—their unapologetic dedication to tearing off every shred of themselves and getting down to the truth of who it is they are portraying: the angry wife who gave her all, and is disappointed in herself for not demanding it in return; the singer who depended on her man to make her a star and took his fists and kicks because she was still grateful to him for believing in her; the college basketball player struggling to hold on to her identity, knowing that doing so flies in the face of the ultrafemme, play-yourself-short, bow-to-the-man narrative society writes for women. When one commits to the truth, it becomes impossible to ignore both the character and her story. It is in that magic where the best stories lie.

I learned the value of committing to my truth from my father, who in my eyes was one of the greatest storytellers of my time. He was unrelenting in his insistence and masterful in his delivery, completely unsatisfied with his work until his audience was whooping and hollering and laughing out loud. It was the embellishing that gave his stories their luster; no matter that he was standing there right in your face, telling a bold-ass, black-ass lie, he committed to building the padding around every detail to really make his listeners think he was telling the truth—even if the subject of said story knew better.

Take, for instance, the time when he convinced my friends that I ate bugs as a child. "I'm telling you! You ate ants!" he insisted, to the howls of a handful of my friends who'd come over to chill for a spell. It's a story I'd heard him recount all my life, but on this particular occasion, at the tender age of twelve, I'd finally figured out that he was just trying to embarrass me, the hallmark of parents' interaction with their children's pals. Life isn't complete unless you take your kids down a peg or two in front of the numbskulls who hold your children in high regard and regularly celebrate their cool factor.

"Daddy, I'm not crazy," I insisted, while my friends, lounging lazily on the swings at the park, continued to laugh. "Are you trying to say I would be sitting in the corner, eating ants that were crawling on the floor?"

"Yeah! You'd be eating ants!" he insisted. "Deny it if you want to, but I was there. I know what you used to do. You'd pick them up with your little fingers and watch them wriggle around and then pop 'em in your mouth." The story would be embellished, of course, with his acting out the actual eating—this oversized man with the same huge, expressive eyes as mine, pinching his fingers together and scrunching up his nose and sticking out his tongue like some kind of hungry, odd-looking anteater on the prowl for a quick meal.

"Well, what kind of father were you that you let your child get out of your sight to go eat ants?" I asked in mock anger. My friends just laughed and laughed. But Daddy wouldn't let it go. By the time the banter died down, he really had me believing I ate bugs off the floor. Committed. He committed to his story, however absurd.

I'd like to think that this is what makes my own most well-known characters iconic. My secret weapon is the commitment—my dedication to the choices I make as I breathe life into those characters. When my director yells, "Cut!" and we agree to do another take of that scene, and yet another still, I am digging in and layering and sprinkling all kinds of seasoning into the stew that makes up the character, her life, her emotions, her mentality in the moment. All of it.

Consider the scene in the film *Baby Boy* when Jody and Yvette get into yet another fight, this one after she finds an open box of condoms in her car—the one Jody drives while she's at work, hustling to make ends meet for herself and their son. In that heated exchange, Yvette, frustrated, hurting, and embarrassed, screams, "I hate you, Jody!" Now, on the page as John Singleton wrote it, it's simply, "I hate you." But as an actress, I have to commit to the meaning of the words—their intention—not just the words themselves. It was I who had to decide whether Yvette is really saying she hates Jody deep down in her insides, or if she's saying she loves him but hates the way he chooses to love her back, or if she's really saying, "This hurts me more than you could possibly know, but fuck you, Jody. Get your shit and get the hell on," or if, truly, she's saying, "God, I love you, let's go upstairs and make another baby." The words are just words, but the intentions lead to both the action and the reaction, so whichever way I, as an actress, choose to deliver those intentions will dictate how I say it. In the case of Yvette, I decided that she doesn't hate Jody, she loves him, but neither she nor Jody knows how to communicate, so she wouldn't necessarily know how to say, "Listen to me, boy, I have some issues with you and I don't like the way you take my car and leave me. I hate how you treat me." She doesn't hate Jody. She's trying to provoke him and get something from him—his loyalty and trust. He doesn't know how to give that, because, like her, he's a kid stuck in a very adult situation, having to make adult decisions when he's simply not ready to do so. So what does he do instead? He uses his fist to get her to stop yelling at him, and then he tries to quell her anger and sadness by giving her oral sex. This is how kids communicate. A younger actress may not necessarily know or understand this, so it's questionable whether she'd be able to move beyond the page—beyond the words "I hate you." Yvette, then, would have been a caricature—a sassy, thumb-sucking baby mama with no depth. I was able to make Yvette memorable, I think, because I had some mileage on me. I could turn those words around on my tongue and squish them against my lifetime of experience, not only as a single mother but also as a woman who has loved and wanted to love again. And I'd just gone through almost the same situation with my son's father—a reality that I carried like a festering wound that would not heal. My commitment to Yvette and her choices almost broke the real Taraji.

It is important to me to extend that commitment to the character even when the camera isn't focused on her. Some actors give their all when the camera is trained in their direction and they're speaking the words, but they're content to disappear when the focus is on someone else. They almost become as inanimate an object as the painting hanging on the wall, or the props sitting on the table: still, lifeless. This is not my way. No matter if my character is the focus of the scene or somewhere in the background, with no words to speak in that particular moment, I'm bringing it. For my character's sake. For my own sake as an actress who wants to make her characters memorable and meaningful. Consider my portrayal of Vernell Watson in *Talk to Me,* the biopic on Petey Greene (portrayed beautifully and with crackling clarity by Don Cheadle), the controversial Washington, DC, television and radio talk show host. Vernell is a composite of the different women Petey dated during his twenty-year reign over DC radio from the sixties through the eighties, when he died. Because there was no real Vernell Watson that I could call for my research, no auntie or cousin who could tell me her struggles and why she loved that man, I was charged with creating her on my own. I started by considering the time period, studying the civil rights movement, the black power movement, the clothing and hair and attitudes of black folk in urban areas of those times. Watching Blaxploitation movies and episodes of *Soul Train* helped me get my swag right: my Afro wasn't so much a hairstyle as it was a crown; my walk not so much one foot in front of the other as it was a strut—a signal that Vernell owned all of who she was, that she felt and was empowered. And then I got down to the heart of who Petey was, because to understand him would be to understand the type of woman who could love him. I talked on several occasions with Dewey Hughes, Petey's manager (played by the brilliant Chiwetel Ejiofor), who was on set; Dewey was quick to point out that

The headshot.

Posing for Darien Davis. (Courtesy of Darien Davis)

Posing for photographer Erik Umphery. (Courtesy of Erik Umphery)

Me with my best friend, Tracy Jenkins. (Courtesy of Pamela Sharp)

Me and the Glam Squad. (Courtesy of Ashunta Sheriff)

Kerry Washington and me dressed in red. (Courtesy of Ashunta Sheriff)

Hanging out with director Lee Daniels. (Courtesy of Ashunta Sheriff)

*The wonderful Ashunta Sheriff hard
at work on enhancing my glam.*
(Courtesy of Ashunta Sheriff)

A scene from the film Hidden Figures. (Courtesy of 20th Century Fox)

Lounging in pink for photographer Itaysha Jordan. (Courtesy of Itaysha Jordan)

Cookie's Wall. (Courtesy of Bruce Weber)

Braided down for photographer Bruce Weber. (Courtesy of Bruce Weber)

Petey had absolutely no filter—that he would say exactly what was on his mind, with no thought about feelings or repercussions, and being that strong-willed often ran him into walls he couldn't knock down. I concluded that a man that tortured, that outspoken, that sure, could be loved only by a woman equally tortured, outspoken, and confident; her crazy had to match his damn crazy for them to click.

So when you see Vernell in *Talk to Me,* she is always on one hundred, even and especially when she is not meant to be the focus of the shot. In one particular scene in a bar, my character is sitting next to Petey but is meant to be nothing more than background. Still, she's smoking a cigarette and bobbing to the music pumping through the bar's speakers, and when her song comes on, she lets out a "Whooo, heeeey!" like, "That's my jam right there." In that moment, my character is living. She is real. She is filling in the empty spaces and coloring outside the lines to help give a more complete picture.

I revel in being the character—so much more than being the superstar. I do not wish ever to be that actress who has a great personality and is comfortable in her skin but portrays her own personality over and over again on film. Those kinds of actors never disappear in a scene. When it comes to my work, I refuse to be Taraji in makeup.

Of course, making a character iconic requires more than just my commitment as an actress; the magic comes, too, in the collaboration with the director. As the captain of the ship, he or she has to steer the production, but we must trust each other's choices to make that magic possible. To be an actress is to give your insides—your beating heart, your gut, your soul—to another artist, trusting that he or she will protect it and make it look its best. I have to trust the vision. The chemistry has to be on point. There needs to be a certain kind of connection, the kind that is so attuned that I can tell just by the way the director yells "Cut!" whether we'll be doing another take or if I delivered exactly what he or she needed to fill in the most perfect picture.

I enjoyed this type of relationship with the director Craig Brewer, with whom I partnered to create the most perfect Shug in *Hustle & Flow*. I knew we had her when we collaborated on the scene in which my character walks nervously into her man's makeshift studio and sings the hook on his rap single, "It's Hard Out Here for a Pimp." When we filmed the part of the scene in which DJay plays back Shug's vocals for everyone in the room, it was my instinct to have Shug listen to the music while rocking and nervous and then freeze when she hears her own voice. Shug literally stops breathing and sits there gape-jawed, shocked at the sound flowing from the speakers.

"Cut—we got it!" Craig said after capturing the moment. After a beat, he considered what we'd done and decided he needed more. "You know what? This time, put your hand over your mouth when you hear your voice."

"Okay," I said, knowing exactly where he was going with it, without his having to waste even another word explaining. What Craig was looking for was what I'd committed to: portraying Shug as a woman who was smothered, with neither voice nor power in her circumstances. Covering Shug's mouth, then, was about Shug needing to stifle the words, as though she were saying, "Oh my God, that came out of my mouth!" We needed to portray not only her surprise, but also her disbelief in her contribution, and her delight and her pride in doing something that had value. This is to say that the director had an idea, and Shug, in all her innocence and fear in the moment, told me why she was doing it. In covering her mouth, she was amplifying her voice.

It was an incredible collaboration—not just with Craig, but, ultimately, with the audience as well, who understood Shug as much more than just some hood rat with a decent voice. Shug, along with Yvette, *Benjamin Button*'s Queenie, and *Empire*'s Cookie, each take audiences on very specific journeys that leave them thinking about the ride and the person driving it, long after the credits roll. The fans respond to the characters by sitting what they loved about them at my feet. Truly, I'm always thrown by who responds to which characters. I can run across a black girl from Harlem and she'll say, "God, I loved you in *Benjamin Button*!" and I can get the same level of excitement from a bunch of giggly Lebanese girls out shopping in Neiman Marcus, running up to me and yelling, "Argh! It's Cookie! We love Cookie!"

The first time I realized my characters resonated with audiences across racial, ethnic, cultural, and economic boundaries was one particular evening when I was leaving the old Landmark Hotel in Hollywood. There I was, walking toward the valet, my feet a little sore, my eyes heavy from fatigue and pinot noir, when I spotted a small group of handsome white men, all dressed in suits, looking as corporate as they come. I gave them the once-over and one of my best smiles, thinking, *Well, feel free to holler at me!* And then, sure enough, they walked toward me and one said, "Hey! You were in *Baby Boy,* weren't you?"

I grinned. "Yes," I said, totally flattered that they not only recognized me, but also knew me from a flick I completely didn't expect that they would have known, much less watched. Remember, *Baby Boy,* which performed modestly at the box office, was barely a blip on anybody's radar; I was sure that no one outside of a very specific urban (read: black) audience had seen it. It wasn't until it came out on DVD that it got the shine it deserved and became an iconic film, but that hadn't happened yet.

A similar experience occurred when I tested for my first television series, *The Division,* on Lifetime TV. There I was, standing in a room full of white suits—network types who couldn't get any more corporate than in this particular crowd. And one man, Aaron Lipstadt, stood up and said, in all earnestness, "Your work in *Baby Boy* was phenomenal."

Their responses, unexpected but pure and welcome, give me air, and they let me know that my instinct to connect with the audience through my commitment to the truth wins every time.

11
On Being a Black Woman in Hollywood

It was still sticky and warm in New Orleans when we started principal shooting for *The Curious Case of Benjamin Button* in November 2006, and I was miserable. By then, Dad had passed, and my heart was every bit as muddy and broken as that gorgeous city, which was desperately scratching and struggling its way out of the watery grave Hurricane Katrina had mercilessly buried it in just the year before. I was in a serious funk, stewed and served up piping hot with a heap of deeply personal losses and also huge business setbacks—a thorough Hollywood screwing that was, frankly, typical for a black woman trying to make a fair and honest wage in the entertainment industry.

The truth is, I should have been riding high when I got the part as Queenie in *The Curious Case of Benjamin Button.* I didn't expect, really, to get the role in the first place, what with every black actress in the Northern Hemisphere vying for the part. When my manager, Vince, called to tell me the director, David Fincher, wanted to meet, I wasn't really excited by the prospects of sitting in a cattle call of actresses scrapping for the job. Plus, the meeting fell on the day that I was hosting a garage sale at my place, and I was way more into hustling to sell my gently worn dresses, stilettoes, and other personal goodies to raise a little shopping cash for a trip I was taking to Italy than I was jockeying for the gig. I mean, I'd already set up shop: I had my dresses on mannequins and my jewelry and shoes neatly arranged on well-appointed tables, and even an area with entire ensembles configured for shoppers who may not have immediately seen the value of purchasing more than an item or two. I even had champagne and orange juice chilling in the refrigerator, and donuts, too, because sugar and mimosas make prospective buyers linger longer, which would only increase my bottom line. Vince's repeated phone calls ordering me down to Fincher's office were wrecking my garage sale flow.

"But the meeting is going to fall in the middle of my sale," I insisted when Vince called me for what seemed like the tenth time. I ran my fingers over the flyers I'd printed up advertising the sale: one said SELLING EVERYTHING: FROM THE ROOTER TO THE TOOTER! "Besides, why are these people working on the weekend anyway? Don't people take off on Saturdays? Can't they meet with me on Monday?"

"I don't care how many outfits you have ready to sell," Vince said emphatically. "I need you to get over to Fincher's place."

Reluctantly, I sent out a mass email to my friends telling them that the sale was off and went to sleep mad about it. The next morning, I woke up still mad and, with an attitude, got myself dressed for the part. The anger was distracting, but it didn't keep me from focusing on the task at hand: even while I was mumbling and cursing out everyone I could think of for my "predicament," I still knew to keep the makeup off my face, to wear period pieces that would have me looking like the character, and to run my lines so that I could walk into Fincher's office not as Taraji, but Queenie, ready to kill that audition, even if I didn't think I had a snowball's chance in hell of getting it.

Still mad, I hustled myself to the address Vince gave me, fully expecting the pandemonium that comes with the cattle call auditions for which Hollywood is famous. But something, I noticed immediately, was off: I arrived to what clearly was Fincher's office. *Well, this is different,* I told myself as I climbed out of my car and surveyed the driveway. There were only two other cars in the lot, hardly enough to produce the pandemonium I was expecting. When I walked through that door, only Fincher and his casting director, Laray Mayfield, were there. It was me he was looking for—me and me alone. Unbeknownst to me, the casting director, Laray, had already whispered my name directly into Fincher's ear after seeing me in *Hustle & Flow,* insisting that the actress who rocked out Shug's character in the film would make the perfect Queenie. Fincher trusted and believed her, and he'd saved the part just for me.

"Forgive me," Fincher said, "I never saw *Hustle & Flow.* But Laray told me so much about you, and when she put in the DVD of your work, she cried while she watched it with me. She believes in your work."

Flabbergasted by the words coming out of Fincher's mouth, I sat and stared at him, distracted only by Laray's enthusiastic agreement. "Yes," she said boisterously in her thick Tennessee accent, "this is our Queenie!"

I was listening intently, but in my head, I was suspicious. I kept looking over my shoulder toward the door, convinced that any second now, there would be a stampede of actresses ready to reaudition for the role. But there weren't any. Just me. I was being invited to play at a different level that actresses dream of achieving, in a role opposite Cate Blanchett and Brad Pitt. This was real.

I gave myself a quick and silent pep talk: *Get your shit together. This is real. Forget the sale and focus.*

"Taraji, I want you to run a scene for me, just so we can see where you are," Fincher said.

I chose the scene in which Queenie first finds the baby, old and decrepit, abandoned on the stoop of the nursing home where Queenie works. And in an instant, Taraji, the thirty-six-year-old single mom eager to get back to her garage sale, was gone, replaced by an older southern woman holding on to a lonely life, battered and bruised by the trials that came in the segregated South. When I looked up, Laray was crying and Fincher was looking on in awe. "That was beautiful," he said. "So tender."

"Look, you can hire her and make this job easy," Laray shared later after I booked the gig, "or you can look at all of these," she told Fincher, pointing to a pile of DVD audition reels.

Fincher chose the former.

I was ecstatic. Here I was, about to be a bona fide star, with all the accouterments that came with the title. At least that's what it looked like on the call sheet, where I was listed as the third principal actor in the cast. This was a huge role—the first in my big-screen repertoire in which I played a main character in a flick specifically geared toward a mainstream (read: white) audience. I am not suggesting for even a half a beat that this made the gig more important than the work I did in, say, *Hustle & Flow* or *Baby Boy*. But starring in a big-budget Hollywood film opposite box office draws such as Pitt and Blanchett was supposed to come with an entirely different set of possibilities: a bigger budget, a wider audience, more publicity, critical responses that could open more doors for me as an actress, and—glory!—a fatter paycheck. When the movie was released, most of this came to fruition, I'll cop to that. But the last item never materialized.

After I got word that I'd received the part, my manager, Vince, settled down to the business of negotiating my pay and quickly crashed into a veritable concrete wall of "take it or leave it" negotiations that left me juggling the equivalent of sofa change compared with what my costars received.

Both Brad and Cate got millions. Me? With bated breath, I sat by the phone for hours, waiting for Vince to call and tell me the number that I thought would make me feel good: somewhere in the mid six figures—no doubt a mere percentage of what Brad was bringing home to Angelina and their beautiful babies, but something worthy of a solid up-and-coming actress with a decent amount of critical acclaim for her work. Alas, that request was dead on arrival. "I'm sorry, Taraji," Vince said quietly when we finally connected. "They came in at the lowest of six figures. I convinced them to add in a little more, but that's as high as they'd go." There was one other thing: I'd have to agree to pay my own location fees while filming in New Orleans, meaning three months of hotel expenses would be coming directly out of my pocket. Insult, meet injury.

Much ado was made when *Forbes*'s 2015 annual list of the ten highest-paid actors and actresses hit newsstands, revealing the gross pay disparity between the genders. Collectively, the men stashed $431 million into their bank accounts, while the women pulled in $218 million—about half that of their male counterparts, even though the top-earning women were some movie-industry heavy hitters with blockbuster projects on the screen. Rather than uphold that pesky, long-held code of silence about what they get paid, actresses like Jennifer Lawrence, Patricia Arquette, Gwyneth Paltrow, and Reese Witherspoon set it off, with Jennifer leading the charge in an essay that had the entire blogosphere giving her virtual fist bumps for telling it like it is after getting wind of the Sony Pictures email hack that revealed she'd gotten millions less than her male *American Hustle* costars. In her piece, the Oscar-winning *Hunger Games* star blamed herself for "giving up" in her own negotiations out of fear that she'd be labeled "spoiled" or "difficult" for demanding equal pay. "I'm over trying to find the 'adorable' way to state my opinion and still be likable! I don't think I've ever worked for a man in charge who spent time contemplating what angle he should use to have his voice heard," she wrote. "It's just heard."

I understood and respected the messengers and especially their messages. There's no reason that in the twenty-first century we should be having this discussion, but here we are, with women—not just us actresses, but *all* women, whether they run a Fortune 500 company or answer the phones at one—getting paid less than seventy cents for every dollar a man makes, even less if they're women of color. But being a black woman in Hollywood comes with a unique set of challenges that can make comparisons of who made what according to gender feel like folly.

The fact of the matter is that Viola Davis was dead right when she used her historic 2015 Emmy Award acceptance speech to contextualize the discussion on inequities in Hollywood. " 'In my mind, I see a line,' " said Viola, who, in winning the Emmy, became the first African American actress ever to take home the award for best actress in a drama. " 'And over that line, I see green fields and lovely flowers and beautiful white women with their arms stretched out to me, over that line. But I can't seem to get there no how. I can't seem to get over that line.' That was Harriet Tubman in the 1800s. And let me tell you something: the only thing that separates women of color from anyone else is opportunity. You cannot win an Emmy for roles that are simply not there."

She went on to thank a grip of folk—me included—who are working tirelessly in front of and behind the camera to be the habitual line-steppers, bringing an influx of quality work to television with shows like *How to Get Away with Murder, Scandal, Empire, Being Mary Jane, Gotham, Black-ish, Bones,* and the like. Still, while television finally blazes its brilliant path, big-screen projects continue to place black actresses squarely in the margins, with leading roles practically nonexistent and pay for the work that is there as paltry as the opportunities, despite the depth of talent we bring to the table. Consider this: A white peer on the same come-up as me pulled in a half million dollars for an independent movie she got right after she finished a small-budget film that got her similar critical acclaim as I got for *Hustle.* Her movie was neither big-budget nor particularly memorable, but she still got paid. But demanding and holding out for a half million in a much-talked-about film starring one of the biggest stars in the game could have cost me, the black actress who worked alongside her in the same movie that brought her the same accolades, my job. The math really is pretty simple: there are way more talented black actresses than there are intelligent, meaningful roles for them, and we're consistently charged with diving for the crumbs of the scraps, lest we starve.

This is exactly how a studio can get away with paying the person who's name is third on the call sheet of a big-budget film less than 2 percent what it's paying the person whose name is listed first. I knew the stakes: no matter how talented, no matter how many accolades my prior work had received, if I pushed for more money, I'd be replaced and no one would so much as blink. So I took my little check, booked myself a small efficiency suite at the local Embassy Suites, and got my ass on to work.

Let me put this out there: a six-figure paycheck and a three-month stay in a hotel is a very big deal where I come from, and this is never far from my mind today as I move through the world, tucking my A-lister coins in my purse and dropping my luggage at the front doors of some of the finest five-star lodging there is to offer. I know that this didn't have to be, and I'm quite clear that the accouterments that come with being a popular celebrity can be here today and gone just as quickly tomorrow. But damn if I didn't have an attitude sitting up in that dingy room in the Embassy Suites, staring at that kitchenette with the old, dusty microwave taking up all the counter space, trying to block out the noise of the five-member family next door bumping up against the walls and playing their television way too loudly while I tried to get myself prepared to play Queenie. I'd sit on the edge of my bed and stew. I was so bitter and angry about so many things—all of them complicated by my dad's death. I wanted to cop an attitude. Instead, I took it to God. I prayed so hard in that hotel room that my knees were black. And finally, He led me to the mission: make it so they never, ever forget you, and then go claim what's yours.

That's exactly what I did. Instead of wasting that energy continuing to be mad, I used it to build my character into an emotional, no-nonsense but huge-hearted woman who loved big, despite circumstances that weren't ideal for a black woman in the early 1900s, barely fifty years after the end of slavery, in the midst of Jim Crow. Whenever I heard footsteps above my head, or felt unappreciated, or thought about my financial situation, I poured every ounce of that feeling into her. I transferred my sadness to Queenie, too; after all, as a black woman in the segregated South, poor, lonely, barren, and about to wind her way through the Great Depression, she had a lot to be depressed about. *This is how Queenie is living,* I kept saying to myself. *She's in the basement in the corner room under the stairs. The people she takes care of live on top of her head, literally, and they live better than her. This ain't about you. This is not your story. This is about her.* I'd listen to music and lyrics from the era—lots of Louis Armstrong, Fats Waller, Cole Porter, and Bessie Smith—to capture the sentiment and mood of that period, and I'd study, too, how an aging body breaks down, so that I could accurately reflect the ailments of a seventy-year-old woman. And every word of prayer I had in my heart while reflecting on my own life in that room at the Embassy Suites I tucked into Queenie. Those prayers manifested themselves in her eyes and words and even her fingers, which unconsciously but constantly rubbed on and grabbed the simple cross that hung around her neck. I leaned on Him. She did, too.

All that anger I had, all that disappointment, all that bitterness, I ultimately laid it all aside and focused, instead, on the work. When I did that, my performance of Queenie became transformed into a spiritual awakening, not just for me but also the audiences who watched the film and cheered my performance. So many times, my costars, many of them elders in the industry and the kind of Hollywood divas who aren't necessarily generous with compliments, would corner me on set, cup my chin, and say, "You really are something to see. You are it. You're going to get an Academy nomination for this one." Same with the cameramen. I'd be coming out of makeup or running my fingers over the goodies on the craft services table, and invariably one of them would sidle up next to me and say, "You're killing it." Even studio executives were flying in with news that my work had the Academy members buzzing. "It's you," one said. "They're focused on you."

I'd made Queenie—and, by extension, Taraji—remarkable, so much so that I got my first Academy Award nomination, for best supporting actress. I was sleepy and a tad drunk—the remnants of a good time had when I went out with my friend and fellow actress Sanaa Lathan—when my friends began calling with the good news. Going out had been Sanaa's idea; she didn't like hearing that I was anxious and pacing around in circles, waiting for the big announcement that was to take place first thing in the morning, before the sun did its slow rise above the horizon. "You need to go out, baby," she chided after I revealed my anxiety. "You shouldn't be in the house waiting for a call. You should be passed out and woken up *to* the call."

"She's right, Mom," Marcell said, chiming in. "You need to go out. Just go."

Pulling myself together, I put on a cute dress, some hot shoes, and some bright-red lipstick, kissed my son good night, linked arms with my friend, and headed to a club in Los Angeles, a spot next to Jerry's Famous Deli on Beverly Boulevard. Sanaa and I made our own fun, giggling and talking and sipping pinot noir and flirting with some of the patrons there and dancing to our own beat. It was the absolute perfect elixir for my racked, jittery nerves.

A few hours later, I went to bed and fell into a deep sleep. I woke up, blurry eyed, to my ringing phone. It was five in the morning, and my manager was on the other end of the line, yapping incoherently in my ear. I knew from the excitement in his voice to look at the television. Sure enough, there was my name, flashing across the screen: Best Supporting Actress: Taraji P. Henson. I ran around in circles, muffling my screams to keep from waking my son; my dog, Uncle Willie, ran behind me in circles, every bit as excited as I.

The whirlwind of red carpets, media appearances, and international press conferences that would round out the *Benjamin Button* Oscar campaign was extraordinary, a spectacle of five-star glitter and glam. We were charged with drumming up as much publicity as we could to grab the attention of the voters responsible for picking the winners. Let me tell you: everything then was first class and five star, from the hotels and restaurants to the travel and the people, some of whom couldn't have been bothered to see me when I was in the films with the primarily black casts, but who knew my name now that "Taraji P. Henson" was accompanied by "Oscar nominee." I was happy to be there, happy to show up in my pretty gowns with my huge smile and promote the hell out of our movie. After all, I was proud of my work and quite pleased that the Academy had nominated me.

Still, I had to keep my ego in check. This is not an easy proposition in this industry, where people blowing smoke up your ass is social protocol designed specifically to get you high enough to believe your own hype and lose focus of the bigger picture. With a hungry baby bird back in Los Angeles, depending on me to put food in his mouth, keep a roof over his head, and make sure his school tuition was paid on time, I made a point of reminding myself that an Oscar or Emmy or any other fancy award I might earn for my performances, while nice, could never be my end game. They could open a few doors, but they'd guarantee neither success nor financial surplus, nor the meaty roles that stretch and honor the talent, particularly if you're a black woman. Those pieces of metal cannot begin to speak for this gift God gave me and what it personally represents. Only the work does.

This is precisely why I wasn't pressed when, while sitting in that Oscar audience, the cameras trained on my reaction, the announcer said, "And the winner of the Academy Award for best supporting actress is . . . Penélope Cruz!" I was happy for her and totally not sorry for me; my mother was by my side, my grandmother was a few rows back with my manager, Vincent, I was in a room full of my peers, I had on a slamming dress, my hair looked good, my makeup was gorgeous, I was a thousandaire, and I was having the time of my life. Completely unaware of this stance, Brad and his wife, Angelina Jolie, with whom I was sitting, reached over to me after my loss, worried that I might be upset. "Are you okay?" they kept asking.

"I'm fine," I insisted. "Can I get some more wine?"

"Let's go get a shot," Angelina countered. Brad and Angie's support for me during that entire awards season means more to me than they'll ever know.

The day after the Oscar loss, everything was silent. There was nowhere to be. Nothing to do. My phone wasn't ringing. It was as if the entire world had stopped spinning, and everyone who had been sticking a microphone in my face, calling my name, and begging me to stand in the bright lights had completely forgotten about me. I welcomed the solace; nothing made me happier than to take a beat to lay around the house in complete solitude. Still, I smirked just thinking about the hoopla—the farce of it all. On that quiet day, the only person to reach out to me was the director Tyler Perry, with whom I'd partied like it was 1999 at the Prince Oscar party the night before. He called to see how I was doing after the loss, but also to put your girl to work. His offer: a starring role in his 2009 movie *I Can Do Bad All by Myself*, in which I played April, a lounge singer who reluctantly becomes a surrogate mom to her sister's three kids. I was grateful for the work, but even more, I'm grateful to Tyler for putting me on the road to being paid my worth. It was he who gave me a fair wage to star in his movie, which ultimately raised my quote—the baseline pay I could negotiate going into subsequent movie deals. "Get your money," he said. It was because of him—not an Oscar nomination—that I never had to take another movie project at the rock bottom of six figures.

. . .

I'm happy when black women win; the significance is important to the whole. If nothing else, Viola Davis's Emmy win for her role as Annalise Keating in *How to Get Away with Murder* got that "first black woman to ever win" thing out of the way so that everybody could stop harping on it as if badass actresses like Viola, Regina King, Kerry Washington, Gabrielle Union, Sanaa Lathan, Regina Hall, Jada Pinkett Smith, Nia Long, Angela Bassett, Vivica Fox, and the like haven't been here, grinding and putting it down on television and film while the industry collectively slept on our skills. Perhaps what was most important about Viola's win was her lifting her voice on our behalf, insisting that Hollywood follow in the footsteps of showrunners like Shonda Rhimes and Lee Daniels in opening its eyes—and its scripts—to the physical, emotional, mental, and social complexities of black womanhood and all the possibilities that lie in its exploration. Consider how Viola devoured the meatiest parts of her role: she showed that a dark-skinned African American woman could be sexy and sexual, cunning and conniving, slick and brilliant and all kinds of evil, and, between all of those loud moments, deeply vulnerable.

I was at my place, trying to rest up from my hectic schedule filming *Empire,* when I grabbed myself a glass of red wine and caught up on the episode in which Viola thoroughly turned out the *How to Get Away with Murder* audience in her iconic scene— the one in which she sits down in front of a huge mirror in her dimly lit bedroom and slowly peels off first her wig and then her false eyelashes, and then wipes away every bit of her makeup until she sits there barefaced, having a real-woman, totally stripped-down private moment in the most public of arenas: national television. I'm here to say, right hand held high, that her work that night was so thoughtful, so truthful, so damn genius, I rewound the scene over and over again, screaming from my gut each time she finished stripping away her layers and stared at her authentic, natural, beautiful black self in that mirror. She wasn't just looking at her own reflection, she was glowering at us, the viewer, daring us to think and stretch beyond the beauty ideal as defined by the pop culture that is shoved down our throats with practically every flicker of light emanating off the television and film screen. In the vein of our greatest actors, Viola brought intelligence, experience, and even a little pain to the moment, displaying in no uncertain terms that she will never fit into "the standard," and that's okay— not just for her, but for us all. Brava, dammit—that's the way you get it done! Truly, Viola is a gift.

Lord knows it's a message that should be shouted from every rooftop in Hollywood, so that the decision makers can move beyond the stereotypes and actually *see* us black actresses and what we have to offer. Not everyone is going to have the look of, say, a Halle Berry, or the ethnic ambiguity of a Gugu Mbatha-Raw, and they shouldn't, considering the diversity of black women. We are light as your white neighbor and as silky and chocolate as the Congo, thin enough to fit in that double zero and curvy enough to fill out a size twenty-two, stretched tall and really squat, too, with weave down our back and with hair so kinky it'll break the teeth out of a strong comb. Some of us are sweeter than a Georgia peach and as quiet as a church mouse, and a gang of us are loud as we want to be and quick to verbally slit throats. And this is just a small sampling of us. There is no one way to present a black woman; we have a voice and we have the right not only to have that voice but also to see it reflected back at us on the screen.

Of course, this is no easy proposition. Time and again, I've lost roles because someone with the ability to green-light a film couldn't see black women beyond a very limited purview he or she thought "fit" audience expectations. Such was the case when I lost the chance to play a pregnant Russian stripper in *St. Vincent,* the comedy-drama starring Bill Murray and Melissa McCarthy. Theodore Melfi, the film's screenwriter and director, wrote the part specifically for me; he was able to see Taraji Henson outside the box—a black woman playing the gritty girlfriend of a grumpy old white man who, despite his battles with drinking, gambling, and general inappropriateness, ends up becoming a reluctant role model to a twelve-year-old neighbor. I was excited about the part and happily informed Theodore that I wanted it. After all, I'd be acting against two comedic gods in the industry, I was downright inspired by Melissa's ability to stretch outside her funny bones to play a straight, serious role, and I was intrigued by the awkward relationship my character would forge with the grumpy, angry counterpart she'd find in Murray's character. Despite my enthusiasm, the role instead went to Naomi Watts, who went on to earn a Screen Actors Guild nomination for her work. She captured the magic of the role—the stretching into her comedic chops, nailing the physicality of being pregnant and working a stripper pole. It was a meaty gig. I would have loved it. Alas, I couldn't get served at that particular restaurant.

· · ·

That may well be just as the universe intended. After all, I'd asked God to guide me and make it so that I would be able to stretch and evolve in my work, avoiding the pitfalls that could come with being typecast into roles. The *St. Vincent* character was a pregnant prostitute, just like my character in *Hustle & Flow.* Maybe my not getting the role was God's way of protecting me. Or setting me up for something even better. As it goes, Theodore Melfi had another intriguing project that was even more perfect than the first, and he insisted on casting me as the lead in it. In his sophomore directorial project, *Hidden Figures,* I play Katherine Johnson, the brilliant mathematician who, along with her colleagues Dorothy Vaughan, portrayed by Octavia Spencer, and Mary Jackson, played by Janelle Monáe, leaped gender, race, and professional boundaries to undertake one of the greatest operations in American history: the launching and safe return of the astronaut John Glenn into and out of space. I'm ashamed to say that I didn't know anything about Katherine or her accomplishments until Theodore approached me with the role, but once I got my hand on the story, did my research, and actually met Katherine, all I could ask was, "Why didn't I know about her and her accomplishments until now?" Little girls, regardless of race, need to know about and celebrate her, Dorothy, and Mary for their genius. Instead, history has erased them. As it turns out, discounting and forgetting the power of women in general and black women in particular is not the sole province of Hollywood.

· · ·

Perhaps my most meaningful role, though, is that which I've become most known for. Playing Cookie makes me feel as if the women I know, the women I grew up around and grew into, are finally getting some shine—but in a much more nuanced way than what is typically afforded a black actress who plays what could be considered a stereotypical role. I'm not deluded for one second into thinking that there isn't a contingent of folk who speed right past the Fox dial on Wednesday nights, convinced that there's nothing useful to see in Cookie's character, and, by extension, the person who portrays her. Hell, I was scared and leery of her in the beginning, too. But I quickly came to embrace Cookie because she *is,* to some extent, me. I'm that girl with whom everyday woman identifies. I'm that struggle. Hell, I'm the American dream. I didn't go to an Ivy League school, I didn't study at Juilliard, I didn't grow up in a mansion. I came from the goddamn hood and put myself through Howard University. I studied Shakespeare *and* August Wilson, until I made something of myself. That's the story of every girl who goes to work every day, punching in at nine in the morning and hustling home at five in the evening. I'm not some fantasy. I'm tangible. And I bring that realness not only to the screen, where it deserves to be, but also out into the world.

And I do mean the world. I've come a long way since those dark nights in the Embassy Suites where I stayed while filming *The Curious Case of Benjamin Button,* hyping myself up through the anger and vowing to show and prove I had the goods to be considered a top-tier actress. Now the world knows my work as Cookie—not just in the streets of southeast DC, or in Harlem or Chicago and Detroit or Houston or New Orleans or up and down the western seaboard, but on television sets in Germany, Australia, France, the UK, Italy, Poland, the Netherlands, South Africa, China, Japan, Korea, and Hong Kong. Not since *The Cosby Show* has a US drama with an African American cast made it this big outside of America, and I'm riding the wave, pleased as all get-out with what comes with those open arms. I'll never forget the energy of the room when, after screening two episodes of

Empire and giving an hour-long talk to an all-French audience in Paris, Lee surprised everyone by bringing me onto the stage. That thunderous applause, the hooting and hollering and the standing ovation, made me burst into tears. But what was even more heartening was that the audience members really understood my character; they got her. They weren't asking me about Cookie's fashion choices or how she wears her hair or what kind of shenanigans the cast gets into behind the set; they made nuanced, insightful queries into Cookie's psyche. They wanted to know from where she drew her strength and how she managed to stay in prison for seventeen years and come out unbroken. The level of questioning was deep and made clear to me that they didn't just watch the show, they embraced it.

. . .

I've worked hard on the screen, but of late, I'm finding joy working behind the scenes, too. I cut my producing teeth on *No Good Deed,* a crime thriller in which I starred opposite Idris Elba. To me, it was an obvious hit: a handsome, charming stranger gets into a car accident and goes to the home of a lonely mom seeking help; she lets him in, and all hell breaks loose. It was formulaic, yes, but what made the film unique was its stars: two African American leads, which is rare in a crime thriller. Getting *No Good Deed* on the screen was no easy feat; Sony/Screen Gems president Clint Culpepper and producer Will Packer would get behind it only if my leading man was a bankable star. Idris, whose talent and sex appeal come with a built-in audience of rabidly supportive fans, was an obvious choice, but also a hard sell. Our filming was set to start at the same time as when he was scheduled to star in *Mandela: Long Walk to Freedom,* his award-winning role as the late South African leader; as the executive producer, I was tasked with figuring out how to turn Idris's fast no into a slow yes. Let's just say it took some hustling, brutish muscle, and a whole lot of promises made so that I could convince the studio to work around Idris's *Mandela* schedule. But the real work came in convincing Idris himself to cram in the filming of my movie just days, literally, before he took off to work in South Africa.

"But I need you," I begged him in a phone call from my home office.

"I know, darling, but I just can't do it," Idris said firmly, in that British accent that makes the ladies swoon. I was undistracted and undeterred.

"But I set it up so that there are zero conflicts," I insisted. "We'll get it done quick. I'm talking we'll work on the weekends and pull twenty-four-hour days if we have to to get you to your next set on time. I already talked to your studio, and my studio is on board and it's a go. All you have to do is say yes."

When he started in with yet another no, I went into Taraji Single Mom Hustle mode. "Look, man," I said, "I really need this gig, okay? I got a son back home and that tuition is kicking my ass and I can't afford to miss out on this opportunity. I can't do this without you, literally. Come on, work with me on this thing." Yes, I played the mom card.

That was some of the best acting I've ever done, I promise you that. Finally, Idris said yes, and all the stars aligned for our project to film without a hitch, finishing up in just the nick of time for Idris to film *Mandela,* just as I, as the executive producer in charge of bringing in the stars and working with the studio to make the project work, had promised.

I employed a similar hustle when I conceived and executive produced *Taraji and Terrence's White Hot Holidays,* the 2015 Christmas variety show that aired on Fox, the home of *Empire.* My vision of the show was born of two loves: my adoration for all things Christmas, and for Carol Burnett. Something that has not and never will change about me is my fascination with the holidays—the warmth shared between family, the joy of giving gifts and watching faces light up when the wrapping comes off and the boxes are open, the magic that twinkles in the Christmas tree lights, the happiness that even the hardest heart embraces when the season kicks in. The moment I hear Donny Hathaway's "This Christmas," I hop right into holiday mode, plotting and planning with my family over where we'll celebrate together, who will cook which dishes, whom I'm looking forward to catching up with after long bouts away from the ones I love. It's this sentiment that I was tapping into when I dreamed up the idea to do a variety show, styled like that which I enjoyed watching as a child fan of *The Carol Burnett Show.* I had only one mission: to spread Christmas cheer straight through the television, with good music, dancing, and, best of all, laughter. The beauty of my success on *Empire* is that it has opened up some serious opportunities for me to spread wide my talents outside of acting, and Fox was quick to say yes to my idea. The moment I got the go-ahead, I sat at my phone and got down to the nitty-gritty of producing, gathering a group of friends to help me bring Christmas stories, music, and cheer, intertwined with a nod to pop culture and a distinctly African American flavor, to the small screen. The success of the show—tucked in the viewership numbers—makes clear that I was onto something. Executive producing is all right by me.

. . .

None of this would have been possible if, on the set of *Benjamin Button,* I'd held on to that initial bitterness. As always, God was right, and so was my daddy: all I had to do was be patient, shut out the noise, and stay focused, and joy would come in the morning.

12
My Squad

Draped in a fierce black custom Alexander Wang gown on the Microsoft Theater stage, with all eyes on me, my *Empire* co-star Terrence Howard, and that glossy white envelope trembling in my hands, nothing else mattered but the raised bold letters that would announce the 2015 Emmy Award for Outstanding Supporting Actress in a Limited Series. The winner's name sent me into a tailspin; my gasp, buoyed by pure adrenaline and unadulterated excitement for my girl, was as audible as my heartbeat was fast. In that very moment, swallowing my excitement and doing the prim and proper thing was not an option. I needed to scream her name: Regina King.

Regina is my heart; we have not only matured and excelled in this industry together, but our friendship runs deep, deeper than simply passing one another on the red carpet or powwowing on movie sets. Ours is a bond made between two busy single mothers who depended on one another for the thing that matters to us most: the care and keeping of our babies. When Marcell and Ian were school age and Regina and I were juggling parenting with the hectic schedules that came with our burgeoning careers, we banded together to provide for one another some of the inherent support that comes with two-parent households: a helping hand with the logistics of having to be in two places at one time, an understanding ear on which to bounce tricky parenting predicaments, commiseration on the challenges of school, thoughtful discussions on what it means to be a mother raising boys. Fortunately, our sons attended the same school, so we came to count on each other for help when the other was working—taking turns picking up the boys, getting them dinner, shuttling them to afterschool activities and such. If Regina was busy, she would still look out for me and mine, arranging for her sister, Raina, and her best friend, Patty, to watch our boys, and for that and for them I am forever grateful. Knowing Marcell was in good hands gave me the peace of mind I needed to take care of business. Though our boys are now men, Regina and I remain inextricably linked, so much so we share just about everything, even the same housekeeper, Daisse! So when I called her name for that Emmy award, and she strutted her pretty self onto that stage and we got lost in our screaming and jumping and joyful exaltations, my happiness for her was coming from the realest place. I was, am, and always will be so proud of her.

Unbeknownst to me, the embrace Regina and I shared onstage would go on to become one of the most discussed and dissected moments of the 67th Primetime Emmy Awards—that, and the moment I stood and applauded, hugged, and kissed Viola when she became the first black woman to win best actress in a drama, the category in which I'd also been nominated. I woke up the next morning in a plush hotel room, slightly hungover from celebrating both the evening and the huge, historic night for us black actresses, and it seemed the entire media world— newspapers, websites, gossip columns, blogs, and social media— was lit with stories that made me out to be the personification of "squad goals," the cultural catchphrase of 2015 everyone was using to describe the power and magic of friendship. I have to admit, though, I found the collective reaction to my actions odd. After all, isn't this what you do when your friend is winning? Squeal and cheer, hug and fist-bump, giggle and yell, "Yaaaaassss!" as she takes her place in the spotlight and shines in its glow? Where I come from, showing up and out for your girl is a basic tenant of true friendship.

. . .

I learned from the best. When I was a kid, I would get downright giddy when I would catch wind that my mother's sisters and good girlfriends were coming by. They just knew how to have fun: the old-school jams would be cranked up on the stereo, and they'd sip their wine while they told stories, worked together on sewing projects, flower arrangements, crocheting, and a bunch of other crafts, and laughed from the very bottom of their guts until well after the moon rose to its heights and the stars were shining their brightest. I had to remain inconspicuous; the adults in the room were from a generation that firmly believed that children were to be seen, not heard, and that little people better not even *think* about getting mixed up in grown-folk business. But the warmth and love in the room was palpable; it was evident, even to my immature eyes and still-developing heart that my mother and her friends were there for one another in every kind of way—when they were happy, when they were unsure, when they were lost in love and trying to see their way clear, when the world was on their backs, and when they needed a firm shoulder to lean on.

I didn't realize it when I was little, but my mother's BFFs were modeling valuable lessons for me—lessons on how to be. Watching them, I learned how to enjoy childhood and also how to be a lady. I learned, too, the value of friendship, of creating safe spaces for children and laughter. I lived for my aunties' hugs, their counsel, their approval, their truth. And they gave it—in spades. When I think of the most significant moments in my life—my graduation, the birth of my son, and the saddest day of my life, the burial of my dad—it is their faces that I see, their voices that I hear, their love that I feel. I always knew, even as a little girl but especially as I grew into a woman, that I needed a collection of ride-or-dies like my mom's.

Though my mother showed me what friendship is, it was my cousins who taught me how to practice it. Our bond was sealed on the living room and basement floors of our parents' homes, on my cousin's pallets. Our parents, all very close, would get together and laugh and play and do what grown-ups do when they're having a good time through the wee hours of the morning, and then, invariably, everyone would be too tired to go home, so the grown-ups would find their way to a spare bed, a pullout couch, or a nice cushiony chair, and the kids would toss a bunch of blankets on the floor and snuggle close to one another, giggling and playing until we passed out. We were thick as thieves: we ate together, played together, bathed together, prayed together. If one got in trouble, we all got in trouble. And we had each other's backs.

A friend of my cousin Kim found this out the hard way. Kim is the daughter of my aunt and uncle who when we were kids lived out in the suburbs in a mostly white community that, socially and financially, felt a million miles away from the southeast DC neighborhood where I grew up. The environmental chasm had no bearing on the connection Kim and I shared, though; even with a difference in age (I'm three years older), family composition (she grew up in a two-parent household), and living quarters (she grew up in a house that, to my child eyes, felt bigger than an entire floor of apartments in my urban complex), we were joined at the hip—this close—and of all the cousins, she was the one with whom I spent the most time. I have to admit, I wasn't really feeling her little friends. Though she liked them enough, often I would swoop in, take a bird's-eye view of her relationships, and call it like I saw it: some of the girls she was counting as pals weren't really friends at all. I didn't like how they made fun of her and treated her like she was a second-class citizen in her own home, and I took delight in letting them know this, too, striking the fear of God whenever I entered the room. See, in their eyes, I was a scary menace—the big, bad cousin coming from the hood in southeast DC—and I happily played on their every fear. You messed with Kim, you messed with me.

Such was the case at Kim's birthday party one year. She'd invited a group of girls over for a sleepover, and naturally, I was invited, too. I sat back, eating chips, sipping punch, and stewing as I watched those girls circle around each other, acting like they were better than Kim and, in some cases, even picking on her. One girl in particular, an overweight sloth with a terrible overbite, a pot-belly, and a nasty disposition, seemed to be the ringleader, going out of her way to be extra foul, not at all moved by my cousin's genuine desire to get along or my menacing presence. I had my eye on her. And I was ready.

"I know!" the girl said excitedly after huddling with a few of the girls. "Let's play wrestle!" A chorus of "Yeah!" filled the air as the big girl and a few of her cronies moved the coffee table and chairs out of the way to make floor space for the matches. Finally, when they had it set up like they wanted, the big girl turned to Kim and said, "You and me first!"

Kim, unsuspecting and completely not ready, agreed and got into her wrestling stance, her puny body squared up against a girl who presented like a miniature peach version of the Hulk. Some-one quickly shouted a countdown and, next thing I saw, Kim was flying across the carpet, her bones crashing against the floor, with that big girl right on top. "Ow!" Kim shouted as the girl, using all her weight and brute strength, pinned down my cousin and ignored her pleas to be let up.

I stood from my perch on the chair, put down my punch, wiped the chip crumbs off my hands, and came with it. "Why don't you wrestle me?" I sneered at the big girl, my eyes boring holes into hers.

The room grew quiet save for my cousin, who was whimper-ing under the girl's crushing weight. Big Girl stared me right in the eye as she let Kim up. I could tell she was taking stock of my weight and build, calculating whether she could take me, the big, scary cousin from the hood. She decided she could.

"Okay," she said, squaring up.

The rest of the girls formed another loose circle, jockeying to see the epic match that was about to commence. Our eyes locked as someone counted us in—"Three, two, one!"—and I was off. I went for Big Girl's legs and rolled into them like a bowling ball does twelve pins when it hits the strike. It wasn't pretty, but I took her down; she went flying through the air and splattered across my auntie's shag carpet. The whole room erupted into "Ooooh" and "Daaaamn" as I popped up and stood over Big Girl's body, like Muhammad Ali did Sonny Liston when he knocked him the hell out.

Kim had no more problems out of Mini Hulk. Or anyone else, for that matter—at least while I was around. That's what it was: you don't mess with her, unless you want to dance with the cousin. This is what cousins—blood by relations but friends deep in the heart—do for one another.

The same is true even to this day. My cousins and I remain close and talk to one another most days through a chat thread my cousin Ricky started years ago—may he rest in peace. Every morning, we wake up to a hearty "Good morning!" and positive affirmations to help us get through our day. It is where, some days, the twelve of us vent about family, work, relationships, and the like. I even lay down my Hollywood burdens there. When I hear, "We got you, cuz," I know I can get the air I need to keep flying.

We guard each other's hearts. This was especially true of my cousin Daniel, whom I loved to pieces. He was my road dawg, the cousin who took me to drag shows and schooled me on the ways of down-low brothers who proclaim themselves heterosexual in public but have unprotected sex with other men behind closed doors. It was he who took me to my first all-male gay club, The Mill, in DC. We walked in and I was mesmerized. I was so wet behind the ears; I thought that homosexual men were all snapping fingers and neck swizzles. But this place would blow my stereotypes out of the water. There we were, standing in this club, lights flashing, house music pumping, and the dance floor was full of hypermasculine men dancing on other men—some of them the same dudes who I would see dancing on women at Chapter III just down the street. Daniel took my hand and pulled me to the bar. "Use protection every time you have sex, Taraji," he warned me as we stood there, swirling the straws in our cocktails. "You don't know who these men are out here screwing and what they're bringing to your bed. Condoms! Use them!" I have no doubt that his advice saved my life.

Daniel also taught me how to be a lady. "Look, Taraji, when you're on the red carpet, carry a clutch. I see a lot of women on the red carpet and they don't carry clutches. You put your lipstick in it, your credit cards and ID, a mint or two, a little gloss for your hair, and you're all set." To this day, sometimes when I leave my clutch at home, I feel like I'm disgracing him.

In the same way Daniel was a friend to me, I made a point of being a good friend to him, too. I still get teary eyed remembering when he visited me shortly after I moved to Los Angeles. He had a list of things he wanted to do, and it was my mission to fulfill his wishes, including going together to get our first tattoos and hooking him up with a performance at an amateur drag show. The tattoo part was easy enough, but I wasn't a part of the drag scene. Scouting out a club was pure fun; I found some of the best

clubs in Los Angeles, filled with the most amazingly beautiful
drag queens I'd ever seen—some of them prettier than a lot of
the women I knew. There was this one dressed up like Sade who
looked so gorgeous I had to do a double take to be absolutely sure
she was a man dressed as a woman. I mean, she had it all: perfect, round breasts and a bubble behind so firm you could bounce
quarters on it. I don't know if she was wearing padding or just
blessed to be shaped that way, but damn, she was hot. That would
be the club, I decided, to which I would take my cousin.

Daniel wasn't the least bit nervous about his star turn. He
locked himself in my bedroom for at least an hour, pouring himself into a long, sparkly, red gown and filling his face with the
perfect application of foundation, lashes, blush, eye shadow, and
glossy red lipstick. I gasped when he emerged from the room.

"Damn, bitch, look at you!" I exclaimed.

Daniel spun around, the tail of his dress making a bubble
around his ankles. "I look good, don't I?"

He was strutting across the living room to get another look
at himself in the mirror when Marcell, completely confused by
the entire scene, furrowed his little brow in wonder. "Mommy!
Mommy!" he said, tapping my leg. "Why is Daniel dressed like a
girl?"

"It's Halloween, baby," I said quickly, exchanging a knowing glance with Daniel. "He's wearing a costume. Go on in the
room."

Hours later, Daniel was up on that stage, dancing and twirling
as if his entire life counted on it. A few days after that, Daniel and
I piled into my little raggedy Nissan Sentra and hightailed it over
to a tattoo parlor, where the two of us would get our first ink.

This was much more nerve-racking for us than any drag show spotlight; fulfilling the former wish brought joy, the latter was guaranteed to bring immense pain. Both of us were scared.

"Is this going to hurt?" I asked, settling into my tattoo artist's chair as he sat next to me, poised with the tattoo gun over the section of the small of my back where he'd just drawn a small dove with an olive branch in his mouth. It was the perfect canvas—a place hidden from public view unless I wore a bikini or my shirt accidentally rode up to reveal it. That's how I like my tattoos; each one is a piece of art with messages that are deeply meaningful, hidden in places that are just for me. I've gotten three others over the years, and am plotting a few more; namely, one featuring the names of both my father and son, and another that says, simply, "God is." I'm an old pro now, but in the moments before I was to get the first, the whir of the gun made me and Marcell, whom I'd brought along because I didn't have a babysitter, jump. I looked nervously over at Daniel, who was across the room in another artist's chair, about to get the yin and yang symbol tattooed on his chest, and wondered if he was as scared as I was.

The tattoo artist, no doubt having felt the tremble of many bodies beneath his tattoo gun, looked at Marcell before he answered my question about the pain. "Is that your son?"

"Yeah," I said.

"This tattoo isn't going to hurt you," he said, noting that the pain was much less intense than childbirth. "But it's going to hurt him," he said, nodding in Daniel's direction.

When that needle hit my back, I was like, "Is this it?" The tattoo artist was right: compared with labor pains and pushing a human out of my loins, getting inked was a walk in the park.

Daniel, on the other hand, was shrinking under his artist's needle, crying like a little bitch.

God, I miss him. Only a month or so after our big LA adventure, in January 2007, my cousin passed away. I miss the camaraderie I had with him; he was my heart, and life just isn't the same without him in it. But I am so grateful that we did get to spend that time together as adults, doing what brought him pure, unadulterated joy, completely trusting that I would guard his heart and ride with him, without judgment. This is what true friendship is made of. This is love.

• • •

My girls Tracie, Guinea, Pam, Ptosha, and Jennifer know all my business, though they aren't in the business, with the exception of Ptosha. They know my love and trust for them runs deep, and that feeling is certainly mutual. Our time together looks a lot like that Apple Music commercial in which I am featured alongside Mary J. Blige and Kerry Washington: lots of laughter and commiseration, good food and wine, great conversation, and, of course, music and dancing. We'll lie out on the beach from sunup to can't see on some of those days, and totally live the sloth life in the spa, getting ourselves rubbed and scrubbed into pure peacefulness.

I kicked off this tradition fairly early in my career. On one such occasion, my girls talked me into taking a weeklong jaunt to Cancún, despite my reservations. Know this: to a Californian, trips to Mexico happen so frequently that vacationing there can feel like you've packed up all your stuff just to go hang out in the suburbs of your own city. But my friends insisted and I needed the break, so Cancún it was. "All right," I said reluctantly. "But don't get out there and drink the water."

The trip turned into one long disaster, rife with all kinds of destruction along the way, beginning with one of my girlfriends absentmindedly leaving her fanny pack at the security gate. We were already outside the airport, walking toward the plane, when she realized she'd left it; we all hustled back to the security gate only to find the entirety of her fanny pack dumped out on a small table, and a bunch of security guards rifling through her stuff. The money: gone. And someone was about to stuff her credit cards in his pocket as we walked up.

It was a sign of a disastrous week to come. The very next day, we climbed into our bathing suits and headed out to the beach for a little adventure, quickly deciding that we'd all pile into a banana boat to explore the waters and bask in the sunshine. Not even ten minutes into the ride, the boat turned over and all of us were in the water, swimming with the fishes, gasping for air as we screamed and desperately tried to anchor ourselves to the boat. My one friend, the one with the fanny pack, tried to kill us all to save herself, flailing and pulling us into the water so she could get a firmer grip on the plastic yellow contraption that was holding us up. "Damn, girl, stop pulling!" we yelled. "You have on a life vest, you're not going to drown! Shit!"

We did manage to have some small measure of fun the night before we left; we found some ratchet club in the middle of the city somewhere and had a blast drinking and dancing and acting the fool. We paid for it the next day: everybody, save for me, was sick as hell, throwing up and battling bubble guts, the unfortunate consequences, no doubt, of drinking the water. Piling onto the misery, Ptosha fell off a bridge into a pool of water while running to get to the van. She came to the hotel's front desk, where the rest of us were checking out, soaking wet, just seconds before we were about to get into a waiting van to rush to the airport. She ended up changing her clothes in the backseat of the car while my other two friends took turns throwing up out the window and debating whether they should stick their asses out of it, too, to empty their bowels. That's how sick they were. Exhausted and hungover, I just sat there in my seat, arms folded, eyes half closed, shaking my head. "See? I told y'all not to drink the damn water. Next time, we're going to Jamaica."

. . .

Each of these women gives me exactly what I look for in a friend: Loyalty and trust. The challenge to be a better me. The space to be unapologetically rough, rugged, and raw. I'm not biting my tongue around them, and while I know they won't judge, I can trust them not to tell me what they think I want to hear. They work me, which I appreciate because it leaves the space for me to be me. This is important, because being fake with the ones I love isn't an option—I'm not that girl. I get paid to pretend, but I won't do it in my real-life relationships.

This is what I appreciate about my friendship with the R&B star Mary J. Blige. She and I are kindred spirits; game recognizes game, and I count her among my closest friends precisely because of our mutual ability not only to be our authentic selves, but also to do so unapologetically and in a way that lets women from our backgrounds, who've experienced our same struggles, know that they're going to be all right.

Ours was a friendship that almost didn't happen. The first time I met her, she hurt my feelings so bad, I didn't know if I'd ever recover. This was back in 2000, when I was still a relative newbie to the industry, shortly after I'd wrapped filming *Baby Boy*. John Singleton and I were party-hopping all around town during Grammy week, and I was fresh on the scene, wide-eyed, and excited to be rubbing elbows with bona fide stars. When I spotted her, my celebrity crush, across the room at one of the gatherings, I leaned into John and tried my best not to squeal into his ear. "Oh my God, you have to introduce me to Mary J. Blige," I said, punching and pinching his arm. "Take me over there."

Shaking his head and smirking at my excitement, John took me by the hand and led me over to Mary the way a parent does a child on her way to meet Santa Claus. I was anxious and excited for my moment in her space—a moment I'd been waiting for since the release of her first album, *What's the 411?*. I needed to tell her that she was a salve for all the pain I felt when I was going through the emotional trauma of dating Marcell's father, and that she was the salve for my broken heart when Mark and I broke up. I needed her to know that her album *My Life* was *my life,* lived out loud in musical form, and that when she cried, I cried. I needed her to know that her art inspired me to keep going and that deep down in my gut, she was, and forever will be, my heroine.

When John walked me up to her, I was ready. And then Mary turned around to face me. She was trying to focus on my face, perhaps to figure out if she knew me. I should have known it wouldn't go well, but, starstruck, a tad naive, and completely undeterred, I launched into my soliloquy. "I love you so much, you inspired my work, you got me through so much," I said, barely taking a breath while singing her praises practically at the top of my lungs, over the noisy din of the music and the crowd. I expected her to open wide her arms and tell me to fall in—maybe ask me for my phone number or maybe offer to accompany me on a lunch date so that we could really get to know each other.

Alas, this wasn't to be. When I finally finished gushing, Mary adjusted her clothes, looked me up and down, sucked her teeth, and, with a dismissive wave, turned her back on me.

I was devastated and felt like less than nothing. *Crushed.* I walked around for a good forty minutes, watching her from afar, and then I got weird. *Maybe she didn't hear what I said,* I told myself. *It is loud in here.* I convinced myself that it was actually a really good idea to go back over to her and tell her again how much I loved her, only this time louder.

So there she was, in the middle of the dance floor, doing that Mary dance, when I pushed through the crowd and walked right up to her and reached between her people to tap her on her shoulder. Before I could withdraw my hand, her sister, LaTonya, smacked the crap out of my arm. LaTonya, Mary, and I laugh about it today, but when it happened, I fought back my tears as I rubbed my arm and walked, dejected, to a dark corner on the side of the dance floor. *Ow,* I said to myself. *You're mean and I don't like you.*

Fast-forward to the night of the Grammy Awards a few years later. I was seeing someone in the industry then, and I was accompanying him as a date to the ceremony when we ran into Mary and her husband, Kendu, at the back door, where the celebrities enter and then get ushered to their seats. I froze when I saw her; chalk that up to that time when I was a crazy fan. In my head, I told myself, *Keep your mouth shut, Taraji. Don't say nothing. I still love you, Mary, but I'm not trying to get hit again.* But on this night she could really *see* me. And this time, she rushed over to my space and commenced to gushing: "Oh my God, Taraji! Come here!" she said. Mary folded me into a great big ol' hug, then grabbed my hands and looked me deep into my soul. "You are the bomb! You make people feel stuff. You take us there. You are so real—I feel everything you do."

There she was, my celebrity hero, telling me that my art moved her like her art moved me. What I'd been saying to her that night she dismissed me, she repeated right back. You couldn't tell me anything for the rest of the night; eyes big as cookies, I floated all through the venue, sending up hosannas to the Lord. I must have said "Thank you, God" at least a dozen times.

We wouldn't connect like that again until 2008, on the set of Tyler Perry's *I Can Do Bad All by Myself.* Mary was cast as Tanya, the bartender friend of my character, April, a self-centered lounge singer thrust kicking and screaming into motherhood when she is suddenly forced to raise her sister's three children. While filming in Atlanta, Mary and I became the best of friends, hanging out every evening, going out to eat, sitting up deep into the night, pouring our hearts out over our shared experiences growing up in the hood, being raised by single mothers, our past relationships. As I'd long suspected, we just got each other. And we've been close ever since. We cheer each other on and cry on each other's shoulders, and meet up as much as we can, given our ridiculously busy schedules. You can usually find us in Nobu, with our mutual friends Angie Martinez and Mary's sister, LaTonya, blowing off steam. Our deepest connection comes, though, when we are secreted away, just the two of us, far from the glitz and glamour, kicking back, being just Taraji and Mary. One of my favorite things to do for my friend is to cook for her. She loves my spicy white chicken chili. I make it nice and hot, with white beans, sautéed chicken breast, cumin, jalapeños, and other spices that boost the flavor just the way Mary likes it. Her bowl stays ready. I'm happy to fill it for her, my friend.

. . .

Of all my girls, though, the best friend I may have is Taraji Penda Henson. I've learned to love myself in ways that I simply didn't when I was younger and more concerned about the care and keeping of others than myself. I'm particular about my energy and I'm protective of my heart, not just with men, but also with friends who seek to do more harm than good in our relationships. I'm a lot like my mother in this regard; we're great at maintaining friendships, but when their shelf life expires, we have no problem tossing those expired friendships in the trash where they belong. But what's more, I'm no longer bothered or afraid to spend time solely with myself. That's something that comes with age; the older I get, the more I take delight in solitude. I like being alone with myself. I crack myself up. I dance with myself. I take care of myself. I love myself. I spoil myself. I take my time, and I'm patient with me. Doing so gives me the superpowers I need to be the kind of mother, daughter, friend, lover, and actress I want to be.

Still, I don't think this growth in particular, or my relationship with my friends in general, is something that is headline worthy, fodder for gossip columns, or the stuff of legendary Internet memes, which is why the interest in my enthusiasm for the successes of my fellow actress friends took me by surprise. My friendships are to me what they are—or should be—to so many more women, who build community around the intimate connections they create with those whom they adore. It is within my sisterhood that I find comfort, joy, drama, understanding, love— the same emotional force that so many other women depend on as they find their way in the world and explore what truly makes them happy. Go to any movie theater or restaurant on a Saturday night, or peek into the kitchens and living rooms where women gather, or sip your cocktail on the margins of the dance floor at the club, and you'll see the manifestation of this—that *Waiting to Exhale* kind of friendship that sticks, even when all else seems to be falling apart. This is our way. In that sense, I am not the epitome of "squad goals." I am one in the sum of its parts, doing what we all do to lift, revere, respect, and protect one another.

13

Grown Woman

Some argue that we're living in an age of oversharing. But there are a few circumstances in which we, women in particular and maybe celebrities more than most, prefer to keep to a limited inner circle the times that we feel most vulnerable. Ranking high up there would definitely be that very instant when we enter the hair and makeup room, sit in a stylist's chair, and slowly remove the shades, hat, and head scarf that we use to conceal whatever's going on up under all that cover. Camera-ready faces and hairdos are built by the hands of saints whose anointed fingers perform miracles; they apply the lashes and concealer and those pops of color for the cheeks, lids, and lips, and then top it all off with a few expertly placed bobby pins, a flick or two of that wrist working the flat iron, and a well-placed hairpiece or wig, and we are single-handedly saved from drowning in an ocean of TMZ-style "Check Out How Crazy This Celebrity Is Looking Right Now" gossip posts and Twitter draggings. I salute the hairstylists and makeup artists who get us ready for whatever it is we need to conquer. They are the true MVPs of the industry, and they guard my beauty secrets like the Pentagon does American war strategies.

Not that I look like some kind of monster beneath the MAC lipstick and Cookie wigs. I'm blessed with equal parts "Black Don't Crack" skin and that good Ballard/Henson DNA—the genes that have kept my mother, aunties, and me looking a good fifteen years our junior.

Just before he died, my daddy said, "God's preserving you for a reason."

I giggled. "What am I, a pickle?"

He laughed that easy, hearty laugh, soft like low thunder. "I don't know, but He is preserving you for a reason."

The reason, I now know, is because of my profession. My youthful look has opened doors for me to roles that were written for actresses much younger than me. I was already twenty-six when I scored the role of a sixteen-year-old in the television series *Smart Guy,* and twenty-nine when John Singleton tapped me for the role as Yvette, an early-twentysomething single mom who, because of her youth and inexperience, can't get herself or her relationship with her knuckleheaded boyfriend together. Not much has changed now that I'm on the other side of forty-five, either. Though I work in a business that has casually and callously shut down the career of all too many women long before their beauty has become weathered by time, I've managed not only to reel in meaty parts, but also to grace the covers of beauty, fashion, and women's lifestyle magazines that tend to reserve the spot for subjects who only recently discarded their sippy cups. I look good. And not just for my age, either. On my good days, when I am alone in my own space, barefaced, with my natural hair plaited tight to my scalp and my ninnies hanging free and low, I feel every bit as pretty as I do with a face full of makeup, a fresh weave, and a push-up bra that makes my cleavage salute the paparazzi.

But dig this: nobody needs to see *that* part of me except with my permission. It is a part of my most intimate, treasured space—my most stripped-down self in the element I love, when I'm kicking back and not worried about anything other than which jazz giant is up next on my Apple Music playlist and what story among the pile of scripts on my coffee table will feed my soul. I don't want anyone seeing the basket weave braid patterns I'm wearing under my wigs, no matter how comfortable I am with them, unless they are a part of my clique of close family and friends or my makeup artist and stylist.

This is what I was explaining in earnest to the renowned photographer and documentarian Bruce Weber, the man behind the lens of a multitude of iconic and controversial fashion and celebrity images that span back to the eighties, when he shot a young Richard Gere for Calvin Klein. He has a reputation as a daredevil—an artist who takes his subjects and their viewers on trips that are all at once sexual and sensual, quiet but in-your-face electric, risky, and, on the most provocative pages, a smidge scandalous. I was beyond excited to find out that Bruce would be the photographer to shoot me for a high-fashion spread for *CR Fashion Book,* the biannual style magazine, as inspired by Carine Roitfeld, the global fashion editor for *Harper's Bazaar.* The pitch was to document my "empire" in a series of shots featuring a small army of eye candy, including Jussie Smollett; the baller Michael

Beasley; the music director and bandleader for *The Late Show with Stephen Colbert,* Jon Batiste; and the model Henry Watkins. My mission was to look like a smoldering cauldron of chocolate so hot, it would singe the fingertips of the *CR Fashion Book* readers and melt the screen of anyone who watched Bruce's short documentary of the shoot.

Bruce had something different in mind, though, inspired by something he was not meant to see: my hair *before* I got into the stylist's chair. I had it braided down in a weave pattern, which I tend to keep for a good eight months out of the year to protect my hair from the overstyling that comes with the job; the braids, cornrows that lie flat against my scalp, make it super-easy to switch from wig to wig and look to look without having to manipulate my thick, natural hair, which, surely, would break off from all the heat and styling products needed to keep it camera ready. The only time I take the braids out is to wash and condition my hair, clip the ends, and let it breathe a little to keep it growing and healthy, and the only time anyone ever sees the cornrows is if my braider is putting them in or my hair stylist is fitting me into a wig. But on this particular day, as I was slipping into a myriad of outfits to have them approved by Bruce for the photo shoot, the scarf under which I was hiding my weave braids slipped off my head. That scarf floated to the floor in slow motion and Technicolor, like some kind of bright leaf caught in the sweep of a gentle breeze. My scream was loud and guttural: "Oh my God! Nooooooo!" I knew I looked good and crazy, standing there barefaced with my black-girl weave braids crawling all over my head, so I did what I know to do in the heat of a sticky situation: I played it off. I tipped my head in Bruce's direction and started bragging on the skill of my hair braider Kendra. "Go ahead and look at 'em," I said, smiling extra hard. "Looks like a basket, doesn't it? It's incredible. Kendra's hands are touched by God."

Bruce leaned in, took a close look, and said: "Great! We'll shoot that."

I'm sure my brows, furrowed enough to be a braid in and of themselves, betrayed my horror at the mere thought of being seen like this in front of Bruce, Carine, and all those fine men on our set, much less having the look documented in the pages of one of the fiercest fashion magazines around. But Bruce gave my "What? Oh, no, no, no, no, no!" zero energy. "Your hair is perfect exactly the way it is," he insisted.

"Bruce. Bruce! Hey, Brucey!" I said, snapping my fingers to get him to focus on the words coming out of my mouth. "This is not the hair people look at, you know what I mean? This is not what the world needs to see. When we put the wig on, that's what they see. This is like a wig cap, you know? You don't put this in a magazine."

My pleading was futile; Bruce was nonplussed. "Of course it's perfect for the magazine. It's not about your hair, it's about your face. It's beautiful."

Moments later, Carine walked in and cosigned Bruce. "Yes, I love it! Beautiful! Let's go! Go to makeup."

I immediately broke out in a sweat and started walking around in circles, talking to myself, trying to figure out how to get out of this particular pickle. I mean, I'd just come off of incredible cover shoots with *W* magazine, *Glamour,* and *Allure,* high-fashion beauty bibles. Their work was stellar, and I was honored to represent for black women, who rarely get to see someone who looks like them peeking from mainstream newsstands in such a big way all practically at the same damn time. And now the photographer and the editor in chief of *CR Fashion Book,* a delicious magazine everybody in the fashion industry checks for when it comes out twice a year, was going to see to it that I looked like a plucked, bald rat, slithering around all these fine men? My confidence was being tested that day, and though I'll be the first to borrow from the rapper Bone Crusher in saying, "I ain't neva scared!" the idea of being photographed this way had me shook. I could just see the memes floating across my Instagram and Twitter timelines: my head, looking all kinds of crazy, with the words "When Cookie Gets Her Wig Snatched!" and "When Keeping It Real Goes Wrong" written in bold letters across the top. We women put so much stock into our hair; it is our crown and glory—the perfect punctuation to our style and beauty. Looking like this in the fashion spread, I was convinced, would not end well.

Jussie, bless his heart, was over in the corner, lifting me up with praises—"But you're beautiful! Stop worrying"—and my publicist chimed in with more of the same: "Your face is gorgeous, look at you!" and that was helpful, kind of. But after everyone stopped blowing smoke up my ass, and I did a shot or two of tequila, I forced my mind to stop thinking like Taraji the fashionista and look at the situation like Taraji the artist: "You have to trust the process," I kept saying to myself again and again as I paced. I saw that twinkle in Bruce's eye—that artist's glimmer. He was inspired. Who was I to question his art? I had to approach the photo shoot not as a woman who wanted to look pretty, but as a character, the way I did when I showed up to my *Hustle & Flow* audition looking like a broken-down, greasy dust bucket to win my part as Shug. *Trust the process,* I repeated. *Go there.*

I did, and Bruce's photos are inspired. It was in those moments, when I was bare and vulnerable, that I did some of my best work. It didn't hurt that all those gorgeous men were helping me along, so sweet and delicate in their handling of me. I was most nervous with Beasley because he's a basketball player; I know the kinds of girls he likes looking at, and you can best believe they're not prancing around him in sew-in weave braid patterns. Earlier he'd been gushing about seeing all my movies, and now he was sitting next to me in the hair and makeup room, seeing me this way. Working through that was tough. "I feel so raw, exposed," I told him.

"You're beautiful. Look at you!" he said. "We men don't care about all that hair. This is what we want to see."

I didn't realize it at first, but Bruce was on the side, his camera primed to capture those intimate moments. "Get in his lap," Bruce said, looking up from his camera. "Sit in his lap and keep talking like that."

We went for it, laughing and flirting and resting in the silence between the words, his hands on my waist and back, mine on his face and neck, the two of us looking like lovers, connecting, sharing. Primed. I was blushing and giggling; he was grinning. And every bit of that emotion, you see in those photos. Bruce caught it all, and we sizzled on both the page and the screen, shot with vintage film and very little retouching. The same is true of a picture Bruce captured while we were walking down the local streets, picking random places to pose and create: we found one shot against the wall in an office building, where a bunch of Czech Americans were working. There they were, banging it out on their computers, completely oblivious to Bruce, his camera, and me, and just beyond them was a wall that, as if by some magic or kismet, had the word COOKIE scrawled across it in some kind of old-world font.

There was no laughing at my hair or those pictures—no backlash or Internet disses. When the magazine published, I saw those gorgeous pictures and thanked God for convincing me not to control the process—to be okay not just with the art, but also with me, in my most natural state, exactly as I am.

. . .

As a black woman who looks like an everyday, 'round-the-way girl, squeezing myself into some teeny-weeny box designed to appease the white gaze was never my thing. I knew girls of color who wanted the fame so bad that they thought they had to starve themselves or have their thighs shaved down to fit in, but most of the rest of us knew that back home, nobody is checking for the skinny girl, and up on the screen, enough of us are representing so that the little girls with chocolate skin and kinky hair and Coke-bottle curves know that they can watch a film or television show and see someone who looks like them. This is why I absolutely loved performing that scene in the first season of *Empire* when Cookie showed her ass, literally, at Lucious and Anika's engagement party. Cookie, under the impression that Lucious is hot for her, climbs into her finest lingerie, drapes herself in a sable fur, and shows up to what she thinks is a private, romantic dinner, only to have to witness her archnemesis gloat about getting a marriage proposal from Lucious. Cookie ends up throwing a fit and storming out the room, but not before flashing her risqué panties. "Oh, and Anika," she snarls, "*this* is an ass." When she says that, Cookie grabs her cheeks and makes them bounce. It's easy to view the scene as yet another outrageous Cookie moment, but dig a little deeper and you unearth its significance: America can't keep thinking a flat ass or an ass plumped artificially is it. Mine is neither tiny nor gargantuan, but a nice-sized, natural one. These kids out there need to see that it is possible to be yourself, love yourself, and win in this industry looking like your natural, beautiful self. Authenticity means something to me, and I make a point of sharing my authentic self rather than pretending to be something I'm not.

Now, I admit I'm luckier than some. Looking younger than I am, and having the wherewithal and energy to work out and eat healthy without giving up the foods that I love or killing myself over a pound here or a wrinkle there is a blessing. It's just as well. I'm so afraid of pain and needles that I don't want to get anything sucked and cut. Hollywood will have you thinking you can have surgery on one day and be up and back to work the next—like it's as easy as picking up a pack of gum and some Newports at the local convenience store. Folks be like, "I'm just going to the store, girl! I'll be back . . . with my new ass." I'm not fooled, not even a little bit. I won't be cutting my way to a skinnier me. What I will do when I'm feeling a little toxic is do a cleanse—twenty-one days of raw, vegan food with lots of vitamins, up to thirty in a day. The older I get, the more I lean toward a raw, vegetarian diet because it makes me feel better, lighter. A lot of my friends are doing this more, too. Personally, I'm inspired by the owner of

Karyn's Fresh Corner in the Windy City, a raw restaurateur who, well on her way to seventy, keeps a cardboard cutout of herself in a bikini by the front door. Her abs and all are right there on display, in case you have any questions about what a raw diet can do for you. I also work out about three times a week with a trainer, but mostly he makes fun of me for being an errant, combative client. I'll head to his gym in my finest workout gear, with a pep in my step, but as soon as I open that door and I see all the machines and equipment and my trainer standing there with his arms folded and his muscles bulging, I revert right back to that little girl who runs around the perimeter of the pool and refuses to touch the water. "Okay, Taraji, give me twenty squats with these weights," he says.

"I'm not doing twenty."

"Taraji, give me twenty," he repeats, as if I didn't hear him the first time.

. . .

You know what keeps me looking young? I laugh a lot. I chill a lot. I'm goofy and silly and I like to have myself some fun. I love feeling the sun on my face and kisses on my cheek. I love good wine and great food, especially if it's prepared by my own hand. I love talking to my son and folding him into my embrace. I love listening to music—jazz especially, but classic R&B and hip hop, too, and, of course, go-go music by some of my favorite DC bands. I love my Jeep Cherokee, the only car I own, because who needs to spend a bunch of money on fancy cars when Uber can get you and your wine from point A to point B without a DWI? Also, I love shopping, especially for shoes and vintage Chanel—

purses, belts, jewelry, jackets, suits, pretty much anything I can get my hands on. I'm a certified Coco Chanel huntswoman; if it exists, I will track it down—in the stores, online, across regions and continents. I have drawers stacked with black boxes that hold treasures I purchased here in America, and white boxes that hold precious goods I scored in Paris. My collection is all at once terrible (because I don't need all these things) and epic (because I need all these things), and I'm sure it's approaching Elizabeth Taylor levels of ridiculousness, but I love each and every piece so hard, it practically hurts.

My attraction to the brand extends far beyond a desire to own expensive goods; it's so much deeper than that. Coco and I go together. She came from nothing—a little orphan girl abandoned at a convent by her father and taught by nuns how to sew, not as a passion but utility, much like how my mother sewed our clothes when I was little. Still, even in that dark place, Coco saw light. She was a dreamer who tossed a middle finger to boundaries—a rebel. I can identify with that. Recently I had the honor of strolling through her apartment and studio in Paris, and felt such a rush breathing in her spirit—the very essence of Coco Chanel. It was such a magical place, filled at every turn with her mystical aesthetic. I lounged on her lush 1920s custom-made suede couch and ran my fingers over the pillows that inspired the quilt pattern in her signature bags, and admired the entryway mirror, marveling at its silhouette, which formed the shape of the Chanel No. 5 bottle. Running up the magnificent spiral mirrored staircase made me giggle as I played hide-and-seek with my reflection in the prisms; that she'd designed the staircase to cloak herself while she observed the genuine reactions of clients and fashion-show audiences was not lost on me. She had a thirst for authenticity, and, along with the luxuriousness of her space, it oozed in every crevice of her home. The black lacquered tables, the chandelier with the trademark interlocking Cs, the Chinese screens with the camellia fleur, the lions and books covered in rich red, all of it made my heart beat fast as I considered the thought she put into every detail of not just the Chanel brand but her own personal being—how all that she knew and loved had value because it meant something specifically to her and no one else. I was particularly moved by the significance of a set of silver charm boxes gifted her by her longtime lover, the Duke of Westminster. The boxes were pretty enough, but the real value lay on the inside, which was pure gold; the tour guide opened it, and it radiated a light brighter than the Fourth of July. To Coco, this was the epitome of luxury: the most valuable and beautiful parts of the boxes—the golden interiors—were special. Something solely for her. You don't show off luxury. Luxury just is.

When I turn that around in my mind, I can make a direct connection between Coco's philosophy on luxury and my attitude toward beauty, art, and even aging in Hollywood. I celebrate the three with passion and great gusto because, to me, they are as natural as the nose on my face and the curve of my hips. No matter how my outer beauty changes or what anyone has to say about it, the true luxury is in my heart, where my gold is, my art and the passion I have for it, which, like Chanel, will never go out of style.

Sure, I'm aging; I'm in my midforties and there are a few more wrinkles now than when I was in my twenties, but when I look in the mirror, I don't see forty-five. I certainly don't feel it, whatever forty-five is supposed to feel like, unless it involves feeling more confident, secure, and primed to do more. I've always felt this way but never more so than when I hit my forties. I'm wiser. Smarter. More reflective. More than ever, I'm motivated.

This attitude was inspired more than fifteen years ago, when I was fresh to the business and struggling while I searched for my next job. I'd scored a few sitcom gigs here and there and even made a star turn in a television movie, *Satan's School for Girls,* opposite Shannen Doherty. But despite a few promising auditions, work had dried up and the devil was on me, stoking my fears and dragging his fingernails through my insecurities. *You old, pushing thirty. Who's going to hire you?* my inner voice questioned. I was scared to even contemplate the answer. It was the hit television show *The Sopranos,* and one of its biggest stars, Edie Falco, who floated me a clue and gave me a crystal ball view into my future. Edie was thirty-six when she starred as Carmela Soprano, the wife of the ruthless but troubled mob boss Tony Soprano and the matriarch of his crime syndicate, and she played the hell out of that part. Saturday night rolled around and anyone who knew so much as my name knew not to call my house while the *Sopranos* was on because, like everyone else, I was gripped by the story and Edie was downright fascinating—not just because her character leaped from the screen, but also because she had surpassed the shelf life of a Hollywood starlet and still managed to earn the respect and admiration of millions. I read quite a few stories about her career and trajectory—hell, at the height of the show, she was being profiled everywhere—and I finally came to understand that no one gave a damn about her age; we were focused on the work, on her talent. We were genuinely turned out by her God-given ability to spin and dig and morph into a conflicted, gluttonous housewife charged with turning a blind eye to her husband's murderous empire, all while reaping the benefits of the dirty business she could not stand. Every week, Edie was churning out deliciously complicated performances, and I watched in awe. She was my mustard seed—that tiny bit of faith I needed to keep pushing forward, believing that my dream of being a successful actress would come to pass.

Meryl Streep was a mustard seed, too; around the same time that I was clocking Edie, Meryl gave an interview in which she said she'd thought for sure her career would end the moment she turned forty. But there she was, having lived half a century, and getting roles of a lifetime.

You're good, I said to myself after reading their stories and considering their work. All it's going to take is that one right role. You're just one role away.

Not long after that, John Singleton cast me in *Baby Boy.*

Frankly, I'm so glad this level of success came for me in my forties because, really, what would I have done with it at age twenty besides getting caught up in all the material things that come with it? I fall on my knees often and thank Jesus Christ that my career went down the way it did.

On the personal front, I do not regret never marrying. I never even felt the pull to have another baby. I made my gynecologist burst into laughter one visit when, after an examination, he questioned whether I would like to try for a daughter. "You have so many eggs here. You could do this easily."

"I got eggs all day long, huh?" I said, sucking my teeth. "You can take them, honey. Take them for free. I'm done. Shop is closed for business."

When my son is ready for kids, I'll be happy to spoil some grandkids rotten. But there will be no more babies this way.

Being a single mother slowed down my clock and gave me a heightened sense of who could be worked with and who needed to be sent packing, that much I know. That was definitely one of the many perks of having my son; rather than focusing on finding a man so that I could have a baby, I could take my time, examine those frogs under the light, find the warts, and know, for sure, that it wasn't right *before* I settled in and wasted precious time. This I appreciated most of all.

These days, when I date, a whole different set of rules comes into play. I've worked my ass off for all that I have, and if I open my world to a man, first and foremost, I have to make sure he means me no harm. Once I've deemed him safe, I have to deem whether the potential mate standing in front of me is bringing something more to the table. By "more," I don't mean material things. I don't care what car he's driving or how much he's got in his bank account, or how many homes he owns. I have property. I have art. I have my own money. Instead, I'm checking for whether he'll feed me spiritually—if he'll take care of my mind and heart. I want a man who is consistent, who will respect me, who will honor me by giving me his quality time, who is fun and funny and willing to be goofy with me, but who can get serious when it's time to work out our issues, without running away. I need my man to make me feel like he wants to be with me and that he'll be incapable of seeing any other girl in the world, because he will be focused solely on me and what we're building together. I need a man who will call me on my bullshit and not let me get away with it because I'm Taraji P. Henson, the star—a dude who will challenge me to be my better self. I need *that* guy. Because I value love. I cherish it. I want it. Even with that missing piece, nothing can stop me from being so glad for this journey— this long road. I prefer slow and steady.

Let's keep it real, though: I'm still hustling and grinding. I'm not trying to do that part forever. I want to get to that sweet spot where I work when I want to work, engage when I feel like engaging, and live life on my own terms. But first I have to tick off a few items on my list. I have to build an estate on my property in Maryland, a beautiful hunk of land that's been in my family for decades. I bought it with my first big check. Acres of it had been sold piecemeal over the years and a mounting tax debt left it in jeopardy of being seized, but my dad had said on his dying bed, "Taraji, go buy that land. Don't let nobody take it from the family. Do something with it." And so I will. I'll purchase, too, a piece of property on the beach somewhere, in another country. Nothing big and fancy—a bungalow or something cute, where I can really breathe and let it all hang out. Nobody will be checking for me. I'll be surrounded by the things that make me the happiest: my son, my mom, my dog, Uncle Willie, maybe a grandbaby or two to spoil, perhaps a husband by my side (if the fates allow), some fresh air, the light of the sun on my face, and my truth— firm, strong, real. I am open to its possibilities.

About the Author

Taraji P. Henson is an Academy Award– and Emmy-nominated actress who stars as the iconic Cookie Lyon in the hit Fox television series *Empire*, for which she earned a Golden Globe. She is the first African American actress to win the Critics' Choice Television Award for Best Actress in a Drama Series. Her classic film performances include Yvette in John Singleton's *Baby Boy*, Shug in *Hustle and Flow*, Terry in *No Good Deed* (with Idris Elba), NASA mathematician Katherine Johnson in *Hidden Figures*, and Queenie in *The Curious Case of Benjamin Button*, for which she earned a 2008 Oscar nomination. She also starred in the television drama *Person of Interest*. Born and raised in Washington, DC, she is a graduate of Howard University and currently resides in Los Angeles.